Sterling and Welch
advertisement.
(Richard Karberg collection)

The Playhouse Square theaters played a key role in the nation's morale during World War II by entertaining the troops. We dedicate this book to all those who served America during World War II, during conflicts since, and to those who today are once again protecting American interests. *(Tim Ryan collection)*

EUCLID AVENUE

CLEVELAND'S SOPHISTICATED LADY,
1920-1970

RICHARD E. KARBERG & JAMES A. TOMAN

Published by
Cleveland Landmarks Press, Inc.
13610 Shaker Boulevard, Suite 503
Cleveland, Ohio 44120-1592
www.clevelandbook.com
(216) 658 4144

ISBN-0-936760-19-2

LIBRARY OF CONGRESS NUMBER-2002112039

Designed by
John Yasenosky

Printed by
Phillips Brothers Printing
Springfield, Illinois

ACKNOWLEDGMENTS

We are grateful to many people for the help they have given us as we worked on our book about the glory days of commercial Euclid Avenue. Without their assistance and support our efforts would surely have foundered.

We express our thanks to: Albert Ratner for sharing information on what happened to Halle's after the store was sold to Marshall Field; Donald T. Grogan for his information and photographs of the Hanna Building; Thomas Randleman for helping us understand the history of the Cleveland Bonwit Teller store; Rosalyn O'Hearn and George Sell of Nestlé, USA for their information about the Stouffer's restaurants and for permission to include some Stouffer recipes; Shannon Burke for her tour and information about the Cleveland Athletic Club; Scott Witkowski for his help understanding the several transformations of the Hotel Statler property; and to Danny Reiger for details on the Mid-Day Club and Sammy's Metropolitan Ballroom.

We are also grateful to the photographers who shared their private collections with us: Lewis Childress, Jim Spangler, Bruce Young, Jack Muslovski, and Tim Ryan. We thank Paulette Batt for giving us access to her wonderful collection of vintage hat boxes from the stores of the avenue. A special thanks also to the photographers of the old Cleveland *Press*, many of whose photographs have been preserved in the Cleveland *Press* Collection at Cleveland State University.

We thank Chris Woods of Cleveland Public Library for his help; and Bill Barrows, Bill Becker, and Vern Morrison of the Special Collections Division of the Cleveland State University Libraries. Robert Keller and Drew Rolik of Forest City Enterprises have also been of great help.

A very special thanks goes to Dixie Lee Davis who agreed to write the introduction for this book, and who generously shared with us her memories and her collection of Halle's memorabilia.

We thank Dan Burnett and the Lake Metroparks' Penitentiary Glen Nature Center for permission to publish a selection of Halle recipes from their archives. Thanks also to Gerda Lenine who provided another Halle recipe.

We are truly grateful to Dan and Cathy Cook and to Greg and Liz Deegan of Cleveland Landmarks Press for their continuing support all throughout this project.

And we are particularly grateful to Judith Karberg and Jane Hazen for the many hours they spent in selecting and testing the recipes which are included here, as well as for all their constructive criticism and thoughtful editing of the various drafts of our manuscript.

Finally, we thank those many individuals who have encouraged us to tell this story of the days of Cleveland's main street. We hope we have lived up to their expectations.

Richard E. Karberg
James A. Toman
August 2002

INTRODUCTION

When I learned that Richard Karberg and James Toman were writing a book about the particular section of Euclid Avenue where I spent each work day for nearly 30 years, my mind was flooded with memories—wonderful, happy memories of my time with the Halle Bros. Department Store.

Halle's at East 12th Street and Euclid Avenue was at the heart of the exciting area that would come to be known as Playhouse Square. In contrast to today, that section of the upper avenue was brimming with activity and was the center for fine stores and shops, beautiful movie houses, restaurants, night clubs, and impressive office buildings.

Much of the excitement was centered on the stores. First, there was Halle's, the most prestigious name in Cleveland retailing, known for its exclusive merchandise from around the world, for its award-winning window displays, and of course, for the beloved Mr. Jingeling. Across the street, about one block east was Sterling Lindner Davis with its four-story tall Christmas tree and enchanting crystal forest housed in a building that had once been home to the Higbee Company before its move to Public Square.

In the early 1950s, New York's Bonwit-Teller opened its sixth branch store on Euclid Avenue near East 14th Street. Bonwit's featured concave display windows which gave shoppers the feeling they could touch the mannequins. The store's violet shopping bags were recognized around the world.

H. W. Beattie, the city's foremost diamond merchant, was known for its artistic window displays, featuring precious stones. Other favorite shops included Bond's, specialty grocer Chandler & Rudd, Murray Bender Shoes, William Kitt, Likly-Rockett Leather Goods, Zucker's Store for Men, Hough Bakery, and Jones-Russell Florists.

The Cleveland Athletic Club and the Union Club were both important parts of the area. The Cleveland Athletic Club attracted families and offered a wide range of sport activities as well as many dining choices. The Union Club, at East 12th Street, was the prestigious setting

for prestigious people. Originally a place where cultured gentlemen could read and discuss topics of the day, today it is a venue where debutantes are presented to society on the impressive staircase at its entrance.

By day the fashion-conscious ladies of northeastern Ohio were drawn to the area to shop, and at night the area came alive with glittering theaters, restaurants, and nightclubs that formed the core of the city's nightlife.

The Keith Building, the tallest in Cleveland for a time, housed the Palace Theatre, often referred to as "America's most beautiful playhouse." The Allen Theatre was part of the Bulkley Building. The Hanna Theatre, which presented legitimate theater, was in the annex of the Hanna Building on East 14th Street. The Stillman, Ohio, State, and Lake theaters rounded out the string of vaudeville and motion picture houses that were a vital part of the avenue.

The area was also the business home for thousands. The Union Trust Building, which today we know as the Huntington Building, alone housed 6,000 employees, and featured the largest banking lobby in the world when it opened. Another large employer was the Cleveland Trust Company, later Ameritrust and now part of KeyBank. It was headquartered across the street from the Union Trust Building. Its banking lobby featured a magnificent Tiffany dome.

By day or night, diners had many restaurants to choose from, including Halle's Tea Room, famous for its welsh rarebit, fruit salad, and cloud nine pie. Other popular choices ranged from the Colonnade Cafeteria to Clark's, Gazelles, and Stouffer's. The Terrace Room in the Statler and Monaco's in the Hanna Building offered fine cuisine.

Just as Richard Karberg and James Toman's book has rekindled for me many happy memories, may it also remind each of us of the exciting time when Cleveland's upper Euclid Avenue was the place to be.

Dixie Lee Davis
Former Halle's Fashion Director
July 2002

PREFACE

Euclid Avenue, in the period of its glory as Cleveland's elegant main street, reflected the optimism, wealth, and opulence that characterized the city at the dawning of the twentieth century. Cleveland, Ohio, was then a city on the grow, a thriving metropolis, emerging as one of the nation's industrial and commercial powerhouses.

The end of the nineteenth century saw the nation's population burgeoning, a trend that would lead to rapid development of its urban centers. Increased population translated into a growing demand for manufactured goods which fueled the rapid expansion of the factories. In a time when transportation opportunities were limited, the cities which had excellent access to both rail and water transportation were the ones that experienced the most dynamic growth. Cleveland was one of them.

Blessed with these resources, Cleveland, and cities like it, attracted large numbers of people. Some found employment in indus-

try, some worked in company offices, and those who had the capital built the city's industrial and commercial infrastructure.

As the population increased, so did the needs for housing, office blocks, and stores. In a time before the private automobile was commonplace, it made good business sense to concentrate the commercial properties where they could be easily reached by public transportation. In Cleveland, that meant Euclid Avenue, where the next streetcar, usually pulling a trailer car, was always within sight. Keeping the buildings close together was necessary and made for a "walking city," where it was both easier and quicker to get from one business destination to another on foot.

The competition for a good commercial location was pervasive, and it soon swept away the elegant homes that just a few years earlier had been built on what was then the fringe of the city. Cleveland's Millionaire's Row, a stretch of grand homes along Euclid

Euclid Avenue was Millionaires' Row in the late 1800s. Mansions lined the street as seen in this view of the Mather Mansion (still standing) and some of its neighbors. This quiet setting was quickly replaced by commercial activity.
(Richard Karberg collection)

Avenue reaching east to about East 89th Street, rapidly gave way to the new urbanization. The stately homes of the Stricklands, Chisholms, Southworths, and the Witts became the addresses of office buildings, theaters, and department stores.

While today many regret the disappearance of Millionaire's Row, civic leaders at the time did not share this concern, not even Tom L. Johnson, the Cleveland mayor who had a home on the avenue. Most Clevelanders were caught up in the excitement of a new age which was making available opportunities and entertainments previously unimagined.

Cleveland was not alone in this transformation. New York residents saw Fifth Avenue change from a sedate and elegant compound for the Vanderbilts, Whitneys, and other affluent families to the location of hotels, theaters, restaurants, and such stores as B. Altman, Bergdorf Goodman, and Arnold Constable, and to hotels, theaters, and restaurants. Chicago's Michigan Avenue witnessed a similar transformation as Marshall Field and other entrepreneurs brought department stores, restaurants, and theaters to the Magnificent Mile. Department stores such as Simpson's and T. H. Eaton replaced residential areas in Toronto.

The trend was international as well. In London, Oxford Street became the location of major department stores such as Selfridge's and John Lewis, as well as many elegant smaller establishments. Berlin saw the emergence of the Kurfurstendamm as the site of department stores, theaters, and hotels. Even in St. Petersburg, the imperial city of stately palaces, the Nevsky Prospekt

Euclid Avenue at East Ninth Street in 1927 was marked by congestion and traffic. Note the famous traffic control tower in the center of the intersection. *(Jim Spangler collection)*

led from the Winter Palace to elegant shops, department stores, the Grand Hotel Europe, and other business establishments.

The rise of the Euclid Avenue district meant that area residents no longer needed to travel elsewhere to find the merchandise they desired. Clevelanders reveled in their city's main street. It was the focal point of the city and a magnet for the state and the region. Mrs. Vincent Sopinski, mother-in-law of Richard Karberg, said coming to Cleveland in the 1930s was like visiting Paris. She was a world traveler and not given to hyperbole.

Euclid Avenue is best understood as being divided into two segments. Lower Euclid Avenue, between Public Square and East Ninth Street, had developed commercially before the upper avenue. During the era described here some established businesses moved to the upper avenue, and in their place came shops that appealed to people of modest means. Its buildings were sufficiently grand and its stores quite respectable, but this part of the avenue lacked the elegance that marked the upper avenue between East Ninth and East 17th streets.

Upper Euclid Avenue became the locale for what was described as the "carriage trade." The upper avenue appealed to the more sophisticated tastes of those who still lived farther east in the remaining Euclid Avenue mansions, as well as to those who had migrated to the Wade Park section of the city or to suburban Cleveland Heights and Shaker Heights. These more affluent Clevelanders seldom ventured west of East Ninth Street.

For a period of time, from about 1920 and into the 1960s, upper and lower Euclid Avenue, from Playhouse Square to Public Square was Cleveland's shopping center. Its stores and shops rivaled those on New York's Fifth Avenue or Chicago's Michigan Avenue, and its theaters rivaled those of Times Square. It was an era when Euclid Avenue hummed with vitality, when window shoppers crowded the sidewalks, and when the bustle of the big city was clearly evident.

Our story recalls these glory days of Euclid Avenue shopping. Not all the stores or restaurants have been described. Rather, we have selected those which we felt would be remembered by most, and we gave more attention to those places that seemed to us of greater significance for the city and its social and cultural development. If we have slighted one of your favorite destinations on the avenue, we apologize, and hope that at least the description of one of its neighbors will bring back some cheerful memories.

Because the recipes in Cleveland Landmarks Press's earlier books on The Silver Grille restaurant proved popular, we have included a few more here, this

Euclid Avenue was lined with commercial structures. Its prominent place in the city and the region had been well established. This view looks east from East Ninth Street—c. 1930.
(*Cleveland* Press *photo, Jim Toman collection*)

By the mid 1920s construction had created a cavernous look for Euclid Avenue.
(*Bruce Young collection*)

time from the Halle's Tea Room and the Stouffer's restaurants.

The reader will notice that the dates given for the closing of most of the establishments we describe came about the same time, the late 1960s. We mention the closings, not so much to emphasize the end of the era, but simply as a matter of historic record. More important are the memories we have retained and the lessons we have learned from studying this wonderful era.

We have also included a bibliography of books dealing with the history of downtown Cleveland, some of which are still in print, and most available through your local public library.

Our story begins in 1920 when Cleveland was America's Sixth City, and when Clevelanders thought that their White Way was a wonderland, international in scope, luxurious, and fashionable. They were proud to be Clevelanders. We hope as you page through our story and look at the photos and illustrations, and maybe even try one of the recipes, that you will be reminded of the wonderful times that you had on Euclid Avenue, when it truly was the place to be. Hum a few bars of George Gershwin, Irving Berlin, or Cole Porter as you saunter down the avenue with us. Enjoy!

Euclid Avenue was probably never more crowded than it was on Sunday April 27, 1952, for the Parade of Progress which marked the end of streetcar service on the avenue. About 300,000 Clevelanders witnessed the parade that day.
(Cleveland Press *Collection of the Cleveland State University Archives)*

I

UPPER EUCLID AVENUE:

STENO PADS, LEDGERS, & ADDING MACHINES

UPPER EUCLID AVENUE emerged as a commercial and entertainment district during the second decade of the twentieth century. Until then the city's commercial area, including department stores, offices, restaurants and theaters had been concentrated in the West Superior district or along the stretch of Euclid Avenue below East Ninth Street.

At the turn of the twentieth century the area to the west of Public Square as well as lower Euclid Avenue was a teeming business district, with every possible tract of salable land occupied by some type of structure. Communication had a lot to do with the constriction of urban districts. In an era innocent of telephone service, let alone fax, e-mail, or other electronic devices, messengers became important employees. Contracts, business transactions, currency, and legal documents all had to be hand-carried from one office to another. Boys as young as seven years of age were employed to spend their days walking from building to building, up and down flights of stairs, making their pickups and deliveries. There was only so much territory that even an army of these messengers could handle in any given day.

After 1900, advances in communication technology, steel cage construction, and the Otis elevator made feasible structures higher than 10 stories, enabling downtown America to expand significantly. By then Cleveland was a booming industrial and financial center, and it felt the pressure to expand its business district. It was a period of time, prior to electronic calculators and word processors, when letters were written on manual typewriters by an army of typists following dictation taken by an equally large number of stenographers. Accounting required another legion of bookkeepers, adding and subtracting by hand or on awkward mechanical adding machines.

The Lennox, a sophisticated apartment house complex, was not even 50 years old when it was demolished in the early 1920s to make way for the Union Trust (now Huntington) Building.
(Jim Spangler collection)

Such a large body of clerical workers required supervisors and adequate working space. Consequently businesses regarded large quarters essential to efficient operations. In Cleveland the only answer to this need for space was to the east.

One by one the mansions of Millionaires' Row were demolished to make way for office buildings and retail establishments. Cleveland business leaders thought the city's most prosperous citizens would continue to reside along stretches of Euclid Avenue, although farther to the east. Business leaders began to talk of the area between East 9th and East 17th streets as the home for "the carriage trade." The term wistfully implied that these select citizens would travel via carriage to their shopping excursions and park adjacent to the establishments they were visiting. Such convenience was not feasible in the congested stretch of the lower avenue.

The four corners of this new district were anchored by distinctive structures. The northeast corner of Euclid Avenue and East Ninth Street, which had been home to the prestigious Lennox office and hotel block, was cleared to make way for the new home of Union Trust Bank (later Union Commerce, and now Huntington banks). This 20-story structure, with over 700,000 square feet of office space, was the largest office building in the city and the second largest in the country. Its barrel-vaulted banking lobby was the largest in the world. The mammoth building opened in 1924, and was soon occupied by a work force of 6,000. The Union Trust Building was designed by Graham, Anderson, Probst, and White, a

The Huntington Building in 2002 remains one of downtown's most prestigious addresses. *(Richard Karberg photo)*

The Cleveland Trust Bank anchored the southeast corner of Euclid Avenue and East Ninth Street—c.1930. *(Cleveland Press photo, Jim Toman collection)*

firm already famous in its Chicago hometown. The firm would, in a few years, become even more famous for its design of the Union Terminal complex at Public Square (the Terminal Tower; Cleveland Union Terminal; the Guildhall, Builder's Exchange, and Midland buildings; and the Higbee Company Building).

The southeast corner of Euclid and East 9th Street was home to the Cleveland Trust Company. Founded in 1894, the fast-growing bank soon found itself in need of more working space. The bank commissioned the firm of George B. Post and Sons to build its new headquarters building. Completed in 1908, the bank headquarters included a magnificent Greek-style rotunda lobby with a glass ceiling designed by the firm of Louis Comfort Tiffany. In an era when a company's stability and prestige were judged by the ornateness and sophistication of its offices, the setting conveyed a sense of elegance and also served to assure depositors of the bank's financial strength. The basement level of the building held a labyrinth of vaults. These seemingly impregnable features further testified to a bank's stability in an era before federally guaranteed deposit insurance.

The 21-story B. F. Keith Building was one of the anchors at the eastern end of the carriage trade quarter. The Keith Building, designed by the Chicago firm of Rapp and Rapp, opened in 1921 and provided an ingenious answer to the problem of providing a facility that could serve multiple functions.

B. F. Keith was a prominent show business entrepreneur during the vaudeville era. From his offices in New York's Times Square, Keith brought together various acts of now legendary entertainers into what was called a bill. He then marketed this bill to theaters around the country, providing the acts with a travel circuit. After a series of performances in New York, for example, a group might begin its travel with a week in Boston, then move on to Albany, Syracuse, Rochester, Buffalo, Pittsburgh, and so on until it completed the circuit, ending up back at Times Square.

As the popularity of the vaudeville circuit performers grew, so did the salaries that they could command. These salaries were not possible when the performers played in small venues. The partial answer, of course, was larger theaters. The other part of the

The stately interior of the Cleveland Trust Rotunda was intended to assure depositors of the institution's financial strength. *(Richard Karberg collection)*

Seen here is the architect's rendering for the Keith Building at Euclid Avenue and East 17th Street. It would be the city tallest structure when completed in 1922. (*Cleveland* Press *Collection of the Cleveland State University Archives*)

Chicago architects Rapp and Rapp devised an ingenious solution. They designed the office tower fronting on Euclid Avenue, with a lobby that served not only the office building, but which also led to the theater built to the rear of the tower on a parcel of less expensive land. This outer lobby opened onto the theater's grand lobby, which served as the anteroom for the 3,680-seat auditorium. The Keith development thus earned revenue not only from ticket sales but also from office rentals.

This plan allowed for funds to make the theater a truly sumptuous venue, and earned for it the title commonly given to large vaudeville houses of the era: "Palaces of the People." These palaces were frequented by ordinary citizens who often lived in cramped housing and in dreary industrial areas. Cleveland's Palace Theatre was particularly lavish. It was the closest that ordinary folks could come to experiencing the splendor in which the wealthy lived.

The fourth anchor to the upper Euclid Avenue district was the Hanna Building. Commissioned by Dan R. Hanna and opened in 1921, the 16-story sandstone building at the southeast corner of Euclid Avenue and East 14th Street was designed in the classical style by Charles Platt. Like its counterpart Union Trust Building at East Ninth Street, the Hanna Building became the home for many of the city's leading firms in industry, shipping, and finance, as well as the headquarters for the important Cleveland Railway Company. A prominent tenant of the building was the elegant Klein's Restaurant on the main floor. Housed in the complex's East 14th Street annex was the 1,535-seat Hanna Theatre,

solution came from taking advantage of real estate opportunities.

By 1920 Keith and other entrepreneurs were scouting central business districts in the major cities for theater locations. In Cleveland the only prime real estate still available was on Euclid Avenue between East Ninth and East 17th streets, and it was very expensive. If a theater were to be built fronting Euclid Avenue, the high cost of land and taxes would have to be passed along to ticket buyers.

which became the home for many of the city's legitimate productions. While elegant in design, the Hanna differed from the other theaters in the district by having a relatively small and simple lobby.

. Between these four anchors on upper Euclid Avenue was an array of other build-ings, mostly dedicated to the carriage retail trade. Many of them possessed distinctive design quality. Nestled between the business anchors, they played a pivotal role in helping define the spirit of the upper avenue and making it the center of sophistication. It is to these that our story leads us.

The Hanna Building, at Euclid Avenue and East 14th Street, was the home address for some of the city's largest businesses. The Hanna Building shows its Italian-inspired design quite well. (*Cleveland* Press *Collection of the Cleveland State University Archives*)

II

SHOPPING ON THE
UPPER AVENUE

MRS. MINIVER HATS,
FUR CAPES,
&
SPODE
DEMITASSE
CUPS

IN THE PERIOD FROM THE 1920s through the 1960s the upper stretch of Euclid Avenue was the preferred destination point for many Cleveland shoppers. For these Clevelanders strolling through the area was a form of entertainment. Window shopping allowed them to view the wide array of often-luxurious merchandise available within the department stores and smaller establishments which lined the avenue.

Many of these window shoppers were not able to afford the merchandise featured along the upper avenue. Nonetheless, the window displays often beckoned them inside, where even if they did not make a purchase, they still had the pleasure of examining the high-quality merchandise first hand. The salespeople in these stores were usually well trained and knowledgeable. Loyal and long-serving, these sales associates often knew the tastes and personal preferences of their regular customers, individuals who

returned season after season and year after year. Shopping in this milieu was akin to visiting with old friends.

The early part of this era was a time when shoppers dressed up to visit the downtown stores. For an expedition on the avenue, a woman wore a proper suit or dress, along with appropriate coat, hat, and gloves. These items had to be fashionable and properly maintained. A man was expected to wear a suit and hat, along with the "correct" coat as weather dictated. Children who accompanied their parents (children did not come alone) wore junior versions of adult fashions. Occasionally

Bonwit Teller's exotic display windows on Euclid Avenue never failed to fascinate passers by. They were designed by Thomas Randleman. *(Lewis Childress photo, courtesy of Thomas Randleman)*

The attractive appearance of The Halle Building added to the store's overall luster— c.1970. *(Halle Bros. photo, Dixie Lee Davis collection)*

eccentric individuals of means would forsake the proper "uniform," but well-trained staff never wavered in treating them with the requisite degree of politeness. Outsiders, however, were inclined to feel self conscious if not dressed correctly, and individuals who could not afford the "right" outfits might have felt distinctly uncomfortable in the salons of the upper avenue. Yet the salespeople were mannerly ladies and gentlemen, and they treated everyone courteously—if sometimes in a condescending way.

The central focus of shopping on the upper Avenue was the Halle Bros. store at 1228 Euclid. Surrounding the Halle store were many excellent and well patronized stores such as Lindner Coy and Sterling and Welch, but for most sophisticated Cleveland shoppers, Halle's was the chief attraction.

This notion of Halle's as the magnet remained the case even after 1951 when the

This aerial view shows the complex of structures which comprised the downtown Halle store. *(Cleveland Press Collection of the Cleveland State University Archives)*

New York firm of Bonwit Teller opened a store in the former Lindner Coy building at 1331 Euclid. Bonwit Teller offered the most exclusive names in clothing, fragrances, and accessories. It was not unusual for some of the store's wealthiest clients to bring their maids along on their shopping excursions. Many of these shoppers also patronized the Stouffer Restaurant next door, and to accommodate them, management created a direct passage between the two establishments. While discriminating women shopped at Bonwit Teller, in the upper echelon of New York chic, the store remained an interloper, coming late in Euclid Avenue's golden era. Its offerings were limited to a place at the higher end of the price scale. So, while it added to the glamor of the upper avenue, it did not seriously challenge Halle's dominance of the retail trade.

Other national firms, most importantly Peck and Peck and Milgrim's, along with local stores such as Quinn Maahs and Engel & Fetzer, were located in this stretch of Euclid Avenue. These were also well patronized but overshadowed by Halle Bros.

What made the Halle Bros. so special? The store had the right combination of excellent merchandise, wide selection, and social panache. There was a mystique about the store which other stores tried to match but were unable to duplicate.

Halle Bros. began business on Superior Avenue in 1891, and just two years later moved to lower Euclid Avenue at East Fourth Street. The store's claim to a preeminent position among Cleveland retailers, however, really began in 1912 when it moved to its new ten-story building at 1228

Samuel Halle served many years as company president and later chairman.
(Halle Portrait Studio photo, Dixie Lee Davis collection)

Euclid. Designed by New York architect Edward Bacon, the store was marked by an elegant yet sedate terra cotta exterior and interior features which provided the appropriate environment for quiet good taste. Bacon, later famous for his design of the Lincoln Memorial in Washington, D.C., balanced severe classicism with

The main floor of Bonwit Teller was divided into intimate areas tastefully arranged to set off the sophisticated merchandise.
(Lewis Childress photo, courtesy of Thomas Randleman)

proportions and detail that resulted in an attractive and comfortable setting.

It soon became apparent, however, that the new building was not large enough to meet the needs of Halle's growing clientele. The first addition came in 1914 and extended

Kay Halle, left, and Kay Richards meet at Halle's— c. 1950. *(Cleveland* Press *Collection of the Cleveland State University Archives)*

Halle Bros. furniture department was located in the Prospect-Huron Building in the 1950s. *(Cleveland* Press *Collection of the Cleveland State University Archives)*

the building's frontage along both Huron Road and Euclid Avenue. Then in 1927 the Walker and Weeks annex building, located between Huron Road and Prospect Avenue and complementary to the main store, increased the store's retail space. Although the architects originally planned to connect the two buildings with a bridge across Huron Road, area businesses objected, and instead the annex was connected to the main building by an underground walkway. In the space of only 15 years, Halle's had grown to span three main streets.

The extensive physical plant enabled the store to house a large number of sales departments and service areas. When Halle's had first moved to its upper Euclid Avenue location, it was mainly known for its lines of fine clothing, accessories, and piece goods. The large new facility allowed the store to offer a full range of merchandise, from pins to pianos.

The Halle store also had restaurant services. On the seventh floor was the Italian Renaissance-style Men's Grille, the Colonial and Mandarin rooms, and the Tea Room. Designed by Owen Coughlan in austere neo-classical style, the Tea Room was paneled in English oak surmounted by antique ivory plaster work. Copper lighting fixtures and oak tables with leather-upholstered chairs completed the room's look.

Providing appropriate dining rooms for women was an important part of retailing during the early part of this era. For genteel women, ordinary restaurants were considered declassé, and while hotel dining rooms were appropriate, meals there tended to be elaborate and expensive. Thus the department store tea room and its refined food became a key aspect of upscale retailing.

The tea room was not restricted to Cleveland. Marshall Field in Chicago, John Wanamaker in Philadelphia, and Macy's in New York City also had tea rooms. Restaurant chains soon emerged—Schrafft's in New York, and Clark's and Stouffer's in Cleveland offered tea room fare as well as more substantial meals.

Halle's Tea Room established a tradition which other Cleveland department stores soon adopted. The May Company had a large restaurant, while Taylor's and Lindner Coy had smaller ones. When Higbee's opened its store on Public Square, its Silver Grille almost instantly became a Cleveland favorite.

Halle's Tea Room became a favorite luncheon spot for women shopping the upper avenue. Not only did it have the advantage of location, it also was the place where the Halle women, Kay, Margaret, Jane, and

Ann, and other socialites would frequently lunch. Thus, lunching in the Halle Tea Room meant sharing the space with members of Cleveland's leading families. Of special interest to women were the many programs presented in the seventh floor

The Halle jewelry department was located on the main floor, adjacent to the elevators— c.1940 *(Cleveland Picture Collection of Cleveland Public Library)*

Halle's millinery department was housed in the 1930s art deco settings established by Gilbert Rohde. *(Cleveland Press Collection of the Cleveland State University Archives)*

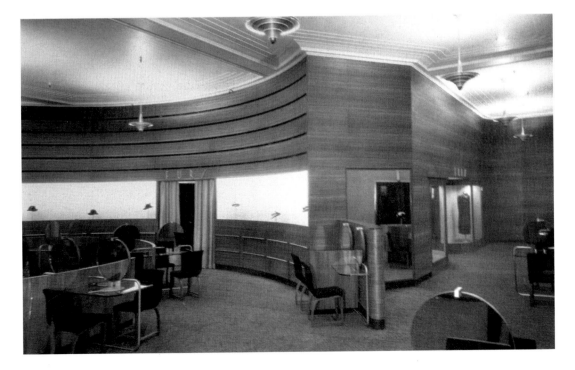

auditorium, featuring food prepared from the Tea Room menu.

Over the years Halle's periodically remodeled the Tea Room. In 1956 Daniel Rassmusson transformed the space into the Minotaur Room. Murals reflecting the style of Picasso and Matisse traced the ancient legends of King Minos. Halle's made sure that brochures were available at the checkout counter explaining the themes of each panel. The next remodeling transformed the space into the Geranium Room. The geranium was a favorite of Blanche Halle, wife of Samuel Halle, and it frequently appeared on Halle packaging and in its advertising copy.

Halle management, recognizing the constraints of time and budget, also maintained an informal luncheonette in the basement store.

While the architecture of the store was distinctive and its amenities appealing, it was probably the staff, and most importantly the Halle family itself, which created the store's distinctive aura. Halle employees were knowledgeable and dedicated to polite and dignified service. Many remained with the store for 25 years or more. The store was

also popular because of the cachet of the Halle name and the family's connection to the Cleveland social set.

The family's connections were both national and international. The Halles worked hard to establish and maintain these connections, and as a result shoppers came to perceive that the Halle store somehow connected them to the glamorous and sophisticated world in which the Halles traveled.

Halle Bros. successfully created this image of luxury and sophistication throughout the store, but certain departments excelled at image making. Book signings from the 1920s into the 1950s brought leading authors from the United States and overseas to the 9th floor book department. Other celebrities were also invited. During the Christmas season in 1934 noted photographer Margaret Bourke White appeared to sell her portfolio. While she was visiting the store, she also took unique photographs of its display windows.

Halle's also perfected its Anglophile image. This preference for Anglo values and culture was reflected in Cleveland social life and could be seen in the development of Cleveland Heights and Shaker Heights with their English Tudor homes, such as the one owned by Walter Halle. The city's clubs had a love of English interior design, including china and fabrics. The English country house life style was quite the fashion, and Halle Bros. capitalized on this market. Authors and other celebrities who came to Halle Bros. typically reinforced this Anglophile point of view.

Probably the best example of this association was the appearance of Sir Harold Nicholson at Halle's in winter 1933. Nicholson was the intimate of British aristocracy, biographer of both King George V and of Queen Mary, and a member of Sir Winston Churchill's cabinet. Nicholson also knew "the bright young things" in English society, a group which included Emerald Cunard, Wallis Simpson, the Duke of Windsor, and Laura Corrigan, who hailed from Cleveland. The appearance of Nicholson and his wife, the author and

famous gardener Victoria Sackville-West, strengthened the notion that Halle Bros. was linked with the highest circles of English society and even associated with the royal family itself. When Sir Winston Churchill, for many Americans the epitome of the English tradition, toured the United States, Cleveland was one of his stops. While in town he was a guest at Samuel Halle's Harcourt Drive home. His visit affirmed the close association of Halle's with the pinnacle of English politics and placed the family at the periphery of the English aristocracy, a connection the Halle family nurtured even after Sir Winston's death.

Samuel's daughter, Kay Halle, exuded an aura of fame and glamour which bolstered Halle's preeminence. Kay Murphy Halle was educated at Laurel School and attended Smith College. After leaving Smith, she began a career as a reporter and moved to New York where her home became a salon attracting some of America's top creative minds. Her association with this leading

A Halle Bros. hat box— c. 1960. *(Courtesy of Paulette's Vintage)*

The boy standing outside a Halle Bros. Euclid Avenue display window is admiring a setting of Lionel electric trains in December 1934. *(Margaret Bourke White photo, Courtesy of Syracuse University Library, reproduced with the permission of the estate of Margaret Bourke White)*

Euclid Avenue displays announced the British Import fair at Halle's in the 1960s. *(Dixie Lee Davis collection)*

Rapid Transit

TIME TABLE
Between Cleveland Terminal Tower and Shaker Heights

SHAKER & VAN AKEN LINES
City of Shaker Heights
DEPT. OF TRANSPORTATION

May - June, 1975

Halle's

HB

Halle's free bus... we pick up where the Rapid leaves off

The Rapid Transit can't come to us, so we do the next best thing. We express Halle shoppers from the Terminal at Public Square right to our doors (and back again) at frequent intervals throughout every shopping day. Convenience that doesn't cost you a penny — that's Halle's for you!

This 1975 timetable from the Shaker Heights Rapid Transit reminds riders of the free connecting bus service from the Terminal to Halle's. *(Richard Karberg collection)*

artistic circle of the 1920s and 1930s is legendary. One summer while away at Halle Farm in Waite Hill, she lent her New York apartment to George Gershwin, who needed a place to concentrate while he was composing *Rhapsody in Blue*. For years her friendship with Randolph Churchill, son of Britain's elder statesman, was a chief topic on the Cleveland cocktail party circuit. Kay Halle wrote, made public appearances, and hosted a radio show broadcast from various settings in the United States and Latin America. For Clevelanders this was indeed a glamorous existence, especially when the accounts of her life were linked to such figures as society columnist Winsor French and Cleveland industrialist Leonard C. Hanna, Jr. This link to café society in New York and to those close to the royal family in England entranced Clevelanders and gave the Halle store the aura of a conduit to a world of glamour and sophistication unheard of in a midwestern American city.

A Halle Bros. purchase, from an expensive piece of jewelry to a plain leather belt, had panache. Gifts from Halle's were beautifully wrapped and delivered by a Halle delivery truck, a signature event which intimated the sophistication and means of the purchaser. Shopping at Halle's put Euclid Avenue on a par with Fifth Avenue in New York, which it imitated.

Halle's reach extended well beyond its downtown store. During the 1920s it opened branches in Erie, Pennsylvania; Newcastle, Pennsylvania; and Canton, Ohio. In the 1940s it also opened branch stores in the Cleveland area: one at Cedar-Fairmount, another at Cedar-Warrensville, and a third at

During the Christmas shopping season, Euclid Avenue remained crowded when the department stores such as Halle Bros. and Sterling Lindner Davis stayed open late—1967. *(Cleveland* Press *Collection of the Cleveland State University Archives)*

Shaker Square. None of these were intended to replace the main store, but rather to tickle the fancy of customers and entice them downtown to see the full array of Halle offerings. When the Cleveland Transit System's rapid transit line opened in 1955, Halle's wisely provided a free shuttle bus service from Public Square to the store.

To attract shoppers downtown, Halle's spent considerable money on renovating its flagship store. It also sponsored many elaborate events, including fashion shows and import fairs. By the 1950s Halle's management recognized that times were changing, and so the company opened full-service stores at the suburban Westgate, Severance, Southland shopping centers, as well as in the Akron area.

By 1970 Halle's sales had slowed, and the family sold the chain to Chicago's prestigious Marshall Field department store. The new owner, however, was not able to reverse the decline that had set in, and in 1981 the Halle chain, then numbering 15 stores in all,

was sold to the Columbus-based Associated Investors Corporation. That transaction spelled the end. The Halle stores were liquidated. The downtown store's last day came on January 27, 1982.

While Halle's was certainly the most well known name on upper Euclid Avenue, other stores brought their own luster to the

A streetcar passes the former Higbee department store in 1945. To its left is the Sterling and Welch building. The two were later joined to become the home of Sterling Lindner Davis.
(Bruce Young collection)

This 1930 Higbee Company advertisement reminds shoppers of the store's fine collection of famous designer clothing.
(Richard Karberg collection)

This 1929 Lindner Coy advertisement helps explain why the store had the reputation of the leading women's shop between New York and Chicago.
(Richard Karberg collection)

area. Lindner Coy was considered the largest ladies' specialty store between New York City and Chicago. Lindner Coy was established in 1908 on East Ninth Street. In 1915 it moved to a distinctive new building designed by Robert D. Kohn at 1331 Euclid Avenue. During the 1920s the store carried gowns by Chanel and offered a wide array of merchandise for women. It also contained a small men's shop, a small tea-room, and a sophisticated gift area at Christmas. Its board of directors included leaders in the clothing manufacturing business at a time when Cleveland was the

third largest producer in the nation. Joseph Biederman of Printz-Biederman served on the board, as did H. Black of the firm of the same name.

Until 1931 The Higbee Company occu-pied premises at East 13th Street and Euclid Avenue and was primarily a store for men's and women's clothing.

Prior to the store's move to Public Square, when the store was owned by the Van Sweringen brothers, other departments began to appear. Like Halle's, Higbee's also appealed to the city's elite. It offered exclusive merchandise with excellent service in a fine

Purchasing hosiery became more brisk at Lindner Coy in 1945 when nylons were again available. *(Cleveland* Press *Collection of the Cleveland State University Archives)*

setting. The store's leadership under the Higbee family and then under Asa Shiverick firmly positioned it as one of the city's most fashionable emporiums.

Higbee's neighbor to the west, Sterling and Welch, also was a frequent stop for Cleveland society. Sterling and Welch carried china, glass, silver, carpeting, and furniture along with other accessories for the home. The store began in 1845, eventually coming under the leadership of Frederick Sterling and George Welch, who in 1902 incorporated the store as the Sterling and Welch Company. Then located on lower Euclid Avenue, the company hired prominent Cleveland architect J. Milton Dyer (also responsible for the design of Cleveland City Hall and the Cleveland Athletic Club) to design a new five-story building on the upper avenue at 1215 Euclid, to which the store relocated in 1909. The new building's most distinctive feature was a glass-ceilinged central court onto which all five floors opened, creating a sense of spaciousness

and sumptuousness.

The Sterling family was a well-established name in Cleveland, and the store was a well-respected institution synonymous with quality and respectability. The wide range of merchandise made it the prime choice in Cleveland for quality home furnishings, a position it held through the 1940s.

Another prominent Cleveland retailer was

The idea of taking tea in the Lindner Coy gown room helped the store convey the image of the amenities shoppers might find at the store. Pictured are Elizabeth Chisholm and Ann Richards—c. 1925. *(Cleveland* Press *Collection of the Cleveland State University Archives)*

A selection of fine furniture is displayed on Sterling and Welch's first floor-1948. *(Cleveland* Press *Collection of the Cleveland State University Archives)*

Trimming the famous Sterling Lindner Christmas tree was a complicated and time-consuming task—1956. *(Cleveland Picture Collection of Cleveland Public Library)*

The decorations for the Sterling tree changed every Christmas season—1952. *(Cleveland* Press *Collection of the Cleveland State University Archives)*

the W. B. Davis Company, a men's clothing store which occupied a position for men's apparel analogous to that which Lindner Coy held for women. Founded in 1879 on Superior Avenue, the store moved to Euclid Avenue, just east of the Williamson Building in 1896. In 1917 it moved a little farther east to a six-story building at 325 Euclid Avenue, next to the Arcade. It remained there until 1947 when Allied Stores Corporation of New York City purchased it (as well as Lindner Coy). In 1949 Allied continued its buying spree by also purchasing Sterling and Welch.

When Allied Stores announced the new Lindner Davis in July 1949, it stated that the merged company was not intended as a department store, but rather as a specialty store patterned after Nieman Marcus in Dallas, Texas, or Saks Fifth Avenue in New York. In 1949, the merged Lindner Davis store moved to the former Higbee Building at East 13th Street. Since 1931 realtors had attempted to find other uses for the former Higbee property. In the 1930s the Garden Center of Greater Cleveland (now the Cleveland Botanical Garden) held the first of its legendary White Elephant Sales at this location, and during World War II the U.S. Navy used the building for its finance office. In 1950 Allied merged Lindner Davis with Sterling and Welch, forming Sterling Lindner Davis. With the adjacent buildings connected, Cleveland had what really was another department store (its sixth).

The new store continued several traditions which had originated in the Sterling and Welch era. The most famous was the Christmas tree which was set up in the central court. The first tree appeared in 1927, and the largest, a 76-foot tall, seven-ton Norway Spruce was put up and trimmed for the holiday season of 1964. The annual Sterling Lindner tree became a Cleveland tradition, and few Clevelanders would consider their holiday shopping complete if they failed to visit and marvel at the beautifully decorated Christmas giant. Sterling Lindner Davis also produced an Easter tree. In 1960 the Sterling Lindner Egg Tree was a 55-foot Sugar Maple, which displayed 1,000 pastel eggs and 2,250 yards of leaf green netting.

These yearly events were Sterling Lindner traditions, and they continued until the store closed on September 21, 1968. The

A Sterling Lindner Davis hat box—c. 1960. *(Courtesy of Paulette's Vintage)*

In this 1929 copy, Sterling and Welch, Cleveland's leading source for home furnishings, advertises its fine selection of decorative objects. *(Sterling and Welch advertisement, Richard Karberg collection)*

ONYX... *a Gift of Rare Distinction*

A GIFT of rare distinction is one of onyx whose rich beauty creates an atmosphere of subtle charm. To those who seek the unusual gift which pays tribute to giver and recipient alike, we suggest a piece of genuine Brazilian onyx. The Main Floor Gallery offers a most complete collection ... in any number of fascinating subjects.

✱

The Sterling & Welch Co.
1225 Euclid Ave.

The Kinney and Levan store was located at 1365 Euclid Avenue. Later the building became the home of Stouffer Foods. *(Western Reserve Historical Society)*

A curving staircase connected the first and second floors of the Kinney & Levan store—c. 1920. *(Richard Karberg collection)*

Kinney & Levan carried not only interior furnishings, but a large selection of lawn and garden accessories as well—c. 1935. *(Kinney & Levan advertisement, Richard Karberg collection)*

The Engel & Fetzer store was a popular women's apparel shop—c. 1938 (*Cleveland* Press *Collection of the Cleveland State University Archives*)

merged operation had not been profitable, and in the absence of any suburban branch stores (Allied had considered opening a branch at the then Richmond Mall—now Richmond Town Center), the Sterling Lindner name passed into history.

Another large store on this stretch of Euclid Avenue was Kinney & Levan at 1375 Euclid Avenue (in what became the Stouffer Building and today is the 1 Playhouse Square Building). The store, which began in 1875, moved to its new building, designed by Walker and Weeks, in 1912. Kinney & Levan featured an enormous selection of household items, including carpeting, furniture, and china. It performed a flourishing wholesale business as well as direct retail to customers. For a time it also operated a budget basement store. In 1932, despite the economic problems the Great Depression was imposing on business, the store expanded its selling space. The move was bold but not prudent. In 1936 the creditors moved in, and the store entered bankruptcy.

One other establishment in the department store category was the Stearn Company.

Founded by Isaac Levy and Abraham Stearn in 1862 at 163 Superior Street, in 1895 Levy and Stearn moved to lower Euclid Avenue. In 1914 the store moved to 1040 Euclid Avenue. The Stearn Company (the Levy name was dropped) originally focused on

Engel & Fetzer carried a large selection of furs, as this 1929 advertisement indicates. (*Engel & Fetzer, Richard Karberg collection*)

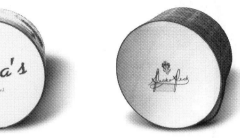

Hat boxes from Engel &
Fetzer, Mary Louise, Cikra's,
and Peck and Peck—
c.1960. *(Courtesy of
Paulette's Vintage)*

household items, especially those which were considered novelties, and on toys in which it took special pride. The toy department featured intricate and brightly colored metal toys from Germany. When the store moved to upper Euclid Avenue, its tradition of an extensive toy department continued, but women's clothing emerged as the featured line of merchandise.

The Stearn family controlled the store until 1945 when Eugene Geismer, Louis Stearn's son-in-law, announced the merger of Stearn's with the national women's clothing company,

Lane Bryant. The store continued to operate as the Stearn Company until 1950, when following extensive remodeling, it took on the Lane Bryant name. Lane Bryant remained there until 1965 when it relocated to 696 Euclid in the former Taylor department store building.

Clustered around the larger stores were a number of exclusive specialty shops which were also noted for the quality of their merchandise and the personal service of their sales staffs. Most of these specialized in women's fashions, but there were also stores for jewelry and men's apparel.

The bright interior of the
Webb C. Ball store brought
extra glitter to the gem
displays—c. 1920. *(Western
Reserve Historical Society)*

We are pleased to announce

A REDUCTION IN THE PRICES
OF STERLING SILVER

ALL prices on sterling silver flatware have been reduced due to the lower price of silver bullion.

This is an opportune time to start a pattern in sterling or add to the one you now have.

There is nothing finer than sterling for gifts and we urge that you get the new prices before buying.

The COWELL *and* HUBBARD *Company*

Home lovers always look forward to our pre-inventory sale.

Rare is the opportunity to purchase fine silver, Royal Doulton, Royal Copenhagen, glassware, etc., at such reduced prices, but such is the opportunity this year.

There are many other lovely things too—at both stores.

The Webb C. Ball Co.
JEWELERS
1112-14 Euclid Ave.   13201 Shaker Square

Several of the women's-wear stores carried exclusive lines of merchandise unavailable in the department stores. Most of these were grouped near the Halle Bros. store, and their proximity to one another made comparison shopping relatively easy. One popular shop was Mary Louise, which opened in the 1930s at 1401 Euclid Avenue and later relocated to 1224 Huron Road. It closed in 1975. Another was Cikra's, a furrier established in 1892. First situated at 1260 Euclid, it later moved to 1242 Euclid Avenue where it maintained entrances on both Euclid Avenue and on Huron Road. The structure which housed the store was eventually razed to make room for the Wyndham Hotel. The store then relocated across Euclid to the former Sterling Lindner Building where it continued to serve its patrons into the 1990s. A third specialty store was Engel & Fetzer, at 1226 Huron Road. It carried regular women's apparel but specialized in furs. It closed in 1967. Peck and Peck was a New York firm which opened its Cleveland store in 1934 at 1315 Euclid Avenue. Best known for its sportswear, it also gained shoppers' attention nationally by introducing the cashmere sweater. It continued on the avenue until the early 1970s.

The Cowell and Hubbard Company carried one of downtown's largest selections of silverware—1930. (Cowell and Hubbard advertisement, Richard Karberg collection)

Advertisement for Webb C. Ball. (Richard Karberg collection)

The B. R. Baker store was the upper avenue's largest specialty store for men— c. 1950. *(Cleveland Press Collection of the Cleveland State University Archives)*

Another group of stores clustered around Halle Brothers were the quality jewelers. In the upper avenue's heyday, these stores carried loose gems with which to design custom pieces. They also featured a large selection of watches, sterling silver flat-

For years the artistry of the Beattie window display has captivated passers by—2002. *(Richard Karberg photo)*

ware and hollowware, and other distinctive works of art, as well as a tasteful selection of gift items. The best known of these merchants was Webb C. Ball, located at 1114 Euclid Avenue from 1910 until its closing in 1961. Ball gained national fame for the manufacture of reliable railroad watches. The large Webb C. Ball clock on the sidewalk, which survives, marks the former site of the store. A second jeweler was Cowell and Hubbard at the corner of Euclid Avenue and East 13th Street. It carried a complete line of Tiffany and Company products, and remained in business until the mid-1970s. Another jeweler was Rudolph Deutsch and Company. Founded in 1894 on Cleveland's west side, it later moved to 1428 Euclid Avenue and then to a location in the Bulkley Building on Playhouse Square.

One jewelry store survived the exodus spurred by suburbanization. The H. W. Beattie Company, founded in 1894, occupied various spots in downtown Cleveland until 1932 when it relocated to 1117 Euclid Avenue, in the Statler Hotel building, where it continues to serve discriminating customers. The store's windows have long awed Clevelanders with their brilliant display of gems.

The largest men's apparel store on the upper avenue's was B. R. Baker. Founded in 1904, the firm moved to 1007 Euclid in 1914 to a building renovated to the designs of Walker and Weeks, Cleveland's dominant architectural firm. Baker's carried all manner of men's and boy's furnishings, but it did reserve one floor for a line of women's apparel. In the 1960s the store was completely remodeled. In 1967 the B. R. Baker Company was taken over by Hart Schafner & Marx, but it continued to operate under its original name. In 1974 it was sold to Hughes & Hatcher, and it took on that name in 1979. The store closed in December 1981.

Not all the stores on the upper avenue were noted for their chic. The F. W. Woolworth Company for many years operated a "dime" store at 1317 Euclid Avenue in another building designed by Walker and Weeks. The store featured two shopping floors offering a full range of Woolworth merchandise as well as a legendary lunch counter. The store opened in 1925 and remained in business until 1974.

Almost all the stores of the upper avenue are now gone, but they live on in memory. They remind us of a time when shopping meant much more than simply making a purchase. The stores connected us to a culture which prized refinement and tradition. They made us feel connected and important.

While the Webb C. Ball store is long gone, its famous clock still keeps time on upper Euclid Avenue—2002. (Richard Karberg photo)

Since 1932 the H. W. Beattie and Sons jewelry store has been at the same Euclid Avenue address—2002. (Richard Karberg photo)

III

DINING ON THE UPPER AVENUE

DUBONNET, WELSH RAREBIT, & WIENER SCHNITZEL

ERIOUS SHOPPING inevitably worked up a hearty appetite, and both lower and upper Euclid Avenue offered a broad array of dining spots, sufficiently varied in ambiance, menu, and price to satisfy any taste or budget.

Among the many restaurants on the avenue, two names stand out: Clark's and Stouffer's. From humble beginnings along the Euclid Avenue corridor, both Clark's and Stouffer's grew into major chains, Clark's into a regional presence and Stouffer's into a national one. Their locations on bustling Euclid Avenue and the success they found there contributed significantly to the growth of both companies. The Stouffer chain in particular catered to the needs of the discerning shoppers who frequented the upper avenue. It offered deft service and refined ladylike cuisine.

The older of the two chains, the Clark Restaurant Company, was founded by J. B. L. Clark in 1896. It began as a lunch counter on Bond Street (East Sixth Street), just off lower Euclid Avenue, and for the next 39 years that was Clark's sole location. In 1935 the Clark Restaurant Company, then led by A. Y. Clark

and R. D. Clark, sons of the founder, was ready for expansion. It then quickly grew to include more than 20 restaurant locations, overseen from the company's executive offices on East 24th Street. Eventually Clark's was purchased by an out-of state corporation, and the new owners closed down the franchise in 1966.

At various times, Clark's operated restaurants at five different Euclid Avenue locations. These were located at 241 Euclid Avenue, 509 Euclid Avenue, 1007 Euclid Avenue, 1520 Euclid Avenue, just east of the Hanna Building, and then finally in the Hanna Building itself.

Clark's Revere House, at 509 Euclid Avenue, only lasted from the 1930s to 1947, but it was an instant Cleveland landmark. *(Cleveland Press Collection of the Cleveland State University Archives)*

Clark's first venture onto Euclid Avenue came in 1935 at 1007 Euclid, just east of the Union Commerce Building (now the Huntington Building) and next to the B. R. Baker Company.

Clark's Colonial at 1007 Euclid Avenue was a popular rendezvous for shoppers, businessmen, and theater goers. (*Western Reserve Historical Society*)

A Clark's menu for October 5, 1953. (*Richard Karberg collection*)

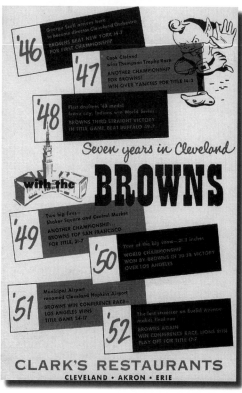

The new establishment quickly became known as Clark's Colonial. Designed in the Georgian style, its two-story facade of white brick and wood was framed by four pairs of double columns, with small flower gardens between the columns. The exterior set the tone for the colonial appointments of the interior.

Just one year later, Clark's opened a second restaurant, at 509 Euclid Avenue in the former Burt's store, and just around the corner from its original home (which the company then closed). Continuing with the colonial motif, the new restaurant incorporated some features from the original Paul Revere house. Inside was a replica of the Revere fireplace, with antique colonial period pistols and rifles fastened to the pinewood walls. Clark's Revere House only survived a decade, giving way in 1947 to a new building for Central National Bank at the corner of Euclid Avenue and East Sixth Street.

Clark's Coffee Shop was located at 241 Euclid Avenue, just east of the Williamson Building, site of today's BP Building and across the avenue and just a little bit east of The May Company store. With a lunch counter as well as tables, the Coffee Shop offered good food, modest prices, and quick service. The coffee shop's appointments were modest, designed for the person on a limited lunch break, rather than for the customer who intended to enjoy a more leisurely meal.

Clark's had another restaurant at 1520 Euclid Avenue in the heart of Playhouse Square which was quite convenient for theater-goers. It operated at that site until 1955 when Child's Restaurant gave up its lease in the adjacent Hanna Building. Clark's then moved into the Hanna space and remained there until 1965.

Clark's cuisine was not fancy. Perhaps the best remembered of its culinary attractions were the homemade pies and ice cream. The traditional favorite was probably the covered apple pie which was served with cheese. In 1930 Clark's commissary trucks carried signage boasting that the chain had served some 700,000 slices of pie the previous year.

Cleveland's other home-grown restaurant chain was Stouffer's, which had two restaurants on Euclid Avenue. Like Clark's, Stouffer's had humble beginnings. In 1922 Abraham Stouffer and his wife Mahala came to Cleveland from Medina and opened a lunch counter in the Arcade. The small business soon had a loyal following, and in 1924, with son Vernon Stouffer active in the business, the family opened its first full-service restaurant in the Schofield Building (now the Euclid-Ninth Tower) at the corner of Euclid Avenue and East Ninth Street. In 1926, Stouffer's moved to larger quarters next door in the Citizen's Building

Clark's also produced a children's menu. This one is from the 1950s. *(Richard Karberg collection)*

Clark's restaurant at Playhouse Square was divided into two areas. One had a more rustic atmosphere—c. 1950. *(Western Reserve Historical Society)*

(now the City Club Building). In 1940 the restaurant moved across the street to 725 Euclid, occupying the first floor of what had formerly been home to the Sherman's and Richman Brothers clothing firms. Before Stouffer's moved, the six-story building was trimmed to two stories and completely remodeled.

The façade of Clark's Playhouse Square restaurant was sharply divided into two segments, suggesting patrons made a decision about which section they preferred prior to entering. *(Western Reserve Historical Society)*

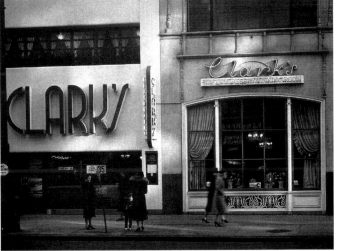

Stouffer's Playhouse Square Restaurant was located next to the elegant Bonwit Teller store on Euclid Avenue, and there was a direct connection between the store and the restaurant. The Stouffer Building (now 1 Playhouse Square) was the former home of the Kinney & Levan department store. *(Cleveland Transit System photo, Jim Toman Collection).*

Unit 1, as the 725 Euclid facility was known, had a weathered oak interior, red draperies, and a wall mural of the Canadian Rockies. In its years there, company officials estimated that the restaurant served 25 million meals. The dining room remained open until November 1977 when it gave way to the wrecker's ball. The site was needed for National City Bank's new headquarters development.

Stouffer's other Euclid Avenue restaurant was located in the heart of Playhouse Square, at 1365 Euclid, on the first floor of the Stouffer headquarters building (the former Kinney & Levan store). This dining room opened in 1936 and quickly was doing a brisk business. As a result, two years later the space was expanded to 19,000 square feet with a seating capacity of 600, making it the largest restaurant in the city. Its theater district location made Stouffer's Playhouse Square the ideal stop for dinner before or after

taking in a movie, and it was also convenient for Halle or Sterling-Lindner shoppers. The restaurant remained open until July 1972. By then gloomy days had descended on Playhouse Square, and the queue of diners had thinned appreciably. The restaurant space later reopened briefly as the Last Moving Picture Company, an eatery featuring large-screen movies and loud music. Designed to appeal to a younger crowd, it was far removed in tone from the sedate ambiance of its predecessor.

The Stouffer Corporation had begun as a restaurant business, but it later expanded into other fields. In 1954 the company launched itself into the frozen food business. It added hotel operations in 1960, and continued to expand its restaurant business into a national chain that eventually numbered 65 units. In many cities the restaurants were at the "top" of one of the tallest buildings (Cleveland's Top of the

Stouffer's operated several restaurants along Euclid Avenue. This interesting menu is from New Year's 1939. *(Courtesy of Nestlé USA, Inc.)*

Happy New Year

DINNER

Tomato Bouillon with Whipped Cream

Two-Tone Cocktail   Frosted Fruit Cocktail

Fresh Shrimp Cocktail

ROAST STUFFED YOUNG TURKEY WITH GIBLET GRAVY   1.25
Cranberry Sherbet

VIRGINIA ROAST HAM, RAISIN SAUCE   1.00

BROILED SIRLOIN STEAK WITH MUSHROOMS   1.50

BROILED LOIN LAMB CHOPS, CURRANT MINT JELLY   1.15

TENDERLOIN STEAK, CHARCOAL BROILED   1.15

Choice of Two

Fresh Green Peas   French Fried Potatoes

Fresh Lima Beans in Cream

Whipped Potatoes   Spiced Young Beets

New Silver Onions in Butter   Candied Sweet Potatoes

and Choice of Salad

Head Lettuce Salad, Roquefort or Thousand Island Dressing

French Endive, Orange and Grapefruit Salad

AN ASSORTMENT OF HOT BREADS AND ROLLS
COFFEE, TEA OR MILK

Minted Ice Cream Meringue, Hot Fudge Sauce

Hot Mincemeat Pie with Sauce   Chocolate Coconut Cream Cake

Dutch Apple Pie with Old English Cheese

Butter Toffee Sundae   Fruit Cup with Frosted Cake Square

Swiss Gruyere Cheese with Toasted Wafers

Luncheon Plates

Cherry Muffin, Raised or Hard Roll
For 20c additional Choice of a 15c Dessert and Coffee, Tea or Milk

Deviled Crab with Tartar Sauce, New Potato Salad,
Tomato Slice 35

Roast Beef Sandwich with Gravy, Pan Browned Potatoes,
Radishes 35

Ham Loaf Baked in Creole Sauce, Pan Browned Potatoes,
Green Olives 35

Fresh Vegetable Plate 35
Carrot Souffle, Julienne Green Beans,
Fresh Asparagus

Breaded Veal Cutlet with Potatoes Hashed in Cream,
Fresh Green Asparagus 40

Baked Lake Trout with Lemon, Potatoes Hashed in Cream,
Tomato Slice 40

A Suggestion

.55

Deviled Crab with Tartar Sauce
New Potato Salad
Tomato Slice
Blueberry Pie

Choice of Freshly Baked Rolls   Coffee, Tea or Milk

Sandwiches

Tuna Fish and Crisp Watercress on Rye Bread 25

Baked Ham on Rye Bread with Mustard Sauce 20

Toasted Sliced Chicken with Homemade Jelly 40

Roast Beef with Fresh Vegetable Relish 25

Deviled Egg and Crisp Watercress on Whole Wheat Bread . .20

Broiled Bacon and Sliced Tomato with Lettuce and Dressing . .25

Grilled York State Cheese with Pineapple Ring 25

We regret we cannot be responsible for lost articles

Afternoon Tea

.35
Choice
Toasted York State Cheese and Bacon Sandwich
Fruit Salad with Toasted Homemade Roll
Assorted Tea Sandwiches
and
Coffee, or Pot of Tea

.25
Choice
Buttered Pecan Bread with Jelly
Cinnamon Maple Toast
Toasted Scones with Orange Marmalade
Ice Cream Puff with Hot Fudge or Butterscotch Sauce
and
Coffee, or Pot of Tea

.45
Choice
Junior Club Sandwich
Sliced Chicken, Bacon and Tomato on Toast
Fruit Salad with Nut Bread Cheese Sandwiches
and
Coffee, or Pot of Tea

Lunch options were always plentiful at a Stouffer's restaurant—1930s. *(Courtesy of Nestlé USA, Inc.)*

Stouffer's offered an "Afternoon Suggestions" menu—1930s. *(Courtesy of Nestlé USA, Inc.)*

Town in the 100 Erieview tower opened in 1964). In 1967 Litton Industries bought Stouffer's, and then in 1973 it became part of Nestlé Food Corporation. In 1990, Nestlé decided to get out of the restaurant business, ending a long-time Cleveland dining tradition. The Stouffer name, however, remains on the company's extensive line of frozen foods.

Playhouse Square was also home to a number of other restaurants. Perhaps the most elegant of these was the restaurant space in the Hanna Building, which over the years was occupied by a number of different operators. Called the grandest dining room between New York and Chicago, it may well have been the space itself, rather than the operator, that made dining at the Hanna seem so special.

The main dining room was designed in the Pompeian style. The center of the room had a ceiling almost two stories high. Along the perimeter were a series of fluted columns leading to other dining and lounge areas. The main room, with seating for 360, provided an almost palatial setting, and its elegance certainly enhanced the dining experience.

Despite the room's grandeur, the restaurant experienced (and interestingly, still does) a significant turnover in operators. When the dining space first opened in 1922, it was under direct control of the building's management and was known simply as the Hanna Building Restaurant. The decision was soon made, however, to turn over the operation to a professional restauranteur. In 1923 Ignatz Klein, who had been operating another downtown restaurant, opened Klein's at the Hanna. Klein operated the restaurant until 1931 when Frank Monaco took over the space. The Monaco era is probably the best remembered. Monaco had style and made his guests feel personally welcomed (much like the atmosphere Gruber's Restaurant in Shaker Heights was later able to achieve). Good dining was accompanied by fine appointments and live entertainment, a combination that made Café Monaco a winner. In 1945 Monaco decided to take a break from the business, but he returned in 1947 with another Monaco's at 1118 Chester Avenue.

The elegant Pompeian setting of Monaco's helped to make it one of the best remembered of the upper avenue restaurants. *(Courtesy of Donald T. Grogan).*

The Continental Restaurant maintained most of the architectural features of the room from the Monaco era, but the lighting was more dramatic. *(Courtesy of Donald T. Grogan)*

Following Monaco's departure, building management again took over the restaurant, operating it as the Continental. Then in 1950 the restaurant was turned over to Child's, a popular New York restaurant chain and one which had earlier

The Continental bar was designed in a sleek modern style, much like the 20th Century Limited and suggested it was designed for serious drinking.
(Courtesy of Donald T. Grogan)

Boukair's was a landmark for lunch, dinner, or after-the-theater treats—1965. *(Cleveland* Press *Collection of the Cleveland State University Archives)*

operated a downtown Cleveland facility. A particular Child's trait was to have one of its chefs flipping pancakes in the front window. Despite that novelty, Child's failed to recapture the old Monaco charm, and four years later, Clark's moved into the space, operating there until 1965 when The Pewter Mug took over.

When Clark's moved into the Hanna Building in 1954, its former space did not long lack a new tenant. The new restaurant at 1520 Euclid was Boukair's Seesweets Restaurant, which became a favorite place to take a date after a movie. Its pastel-colored lighting seemed to tempt the sweet tooth, and Boukair's concoctions did not disappoint. Whether indulging on a huge ice cream sundae, a rich soda or milk shake, or even a tasty dessert cocktail, customers found Boukair's a wonderful place to wind up an evening on Playhouse Square.

The upper avenue was home to a variety of other dining spots which, while not the choice of the carriage trade shopper with tea room taste, nonetheless attracted a loyal following because of their excellent specialized cuisine. They also became places to hobnob with Cleveland's sports and entertainment celebrities and its most fascinating society figures like Winsor French, Kay Halle, and Leonard C. Hanna, Jr. The "jolly set" which patronized these venues were loyal, and many made sure to patronize the restaurant owners' out-of-town ventures when visiting Las Vegas and elsewhere.

Immediately east of Boukair's, at 1524 Euclid Avenue was the popular Pierre's Italian restaurant, named for its founder, Pierre Pieratoni. Following his death in 1945,

Pierre's was taken over by Hector Boiardi (originator of the Chef Boy-ar-dee line of canned spaghetti products), who had been operating Chef Hector's at 823 Prospect Avenue since 1931. Boiardi then joined with Albert Caminati to operate both Chef Hector's and Pierre's. Chef Hector's and Pierre's were favorites of those with a hankering for Italian cuisine, and both establishments had a loyal clientele. Chef Hector's closed in 1967, Pierre's in early 1974.

Playhouse Square also offered Clevelanders a taste of night club life at Herman Pirchner's Alpine Village at 1614 Euclid Avenue. For almost three decades, from 1933 until 1961, the Alpine Village was the Cleveland party center, and rollicking good times were had by all who experienced this Cleveland version of German "gemütlichkeit": good food, good beer, dancing, and music.

Chef Hector's Restaurant was out of the way, hidden behind East Ninth Street buildings, but many people nonetheless found their way to it. (Cleveland Press Collection of the Cleveland State University Archives)

Herman Pirchner's Alpine Village was a landmark. The Edward Winter murals were an important contribution to the Cleveland art world. (Cleveland Press Collection of the Cleveland State University Archives)

World War II was over, and fall 1945 was a time to celebrate at the Alpine Village. Marjorie Hargus (nee Toman), sister of one of the authors, (back row, left) is with a group of friends from the American Steel and Wire Company. Pictures like this were readily available from the Village photographer. *(Alpine Village photo, Jim Toman collection)*

The Italian cuisine at Pierre's was appealing, more so than the modernized facade which adorned its structure-1964. *(Cleveland* Press *Collection of the Cleveland State University Archives)*

Pirchner himself was a key ingredient in the supper club's popularity. He was a master showman, a jovial impresario in lederhosen, who could make his guests feel not only welcome but important as well. The Alpine Village attracted all kinds of people, and it was especially popular with groups who were in party mode. Special events like weddings and after-prom parties were celebrated there, as were more mundane occasions such as birthday parties or bowling banquets.

The club also drew the celebrities who came to Cleveland on Keith's vaudeville circuit, and the Village was a favorite watering hole (and gossip mill) for the reporters of the city's three daily newspapers.

Decor and menu items reflected the Alpine name. One of the club's most distinctive features was a dance floor that could be raised or lowered. If one were so inclined, he or she could begin the dining experience with a glass of sauerkraut juice, followed by a main course of bratwurst or pig's knuckles, complemented by any number of German wines. While the menu did feature these German dishes, typical American favorites predominated. In keeping with its night club identity, the Alpine Village had a minimum cover charge.

The Alpine Village did well right from its start, even during the World War II years when some Clevelanders found its Germanic flavor a bit unpatriotic. By the late 1950s, however, as suburban retail centers and movie theaters began to drain the crowds from Playhouse Square, business began to slow, and in 1957 the IRS padlocked the restaurant for a few months because of tax delinquencies. At this point, Pirchner sold the establishment. The new owners, however, recognizing how much the Alpine Village was associated with Pirchner's name, wisely retained him as the restaurant's general manager. In 1961, the club faced new tax troubles, and it was closed for a second—and final—time that December.

After Alpine Village closed, other operators took over and briefly operated the space. It was the Americana Supper Club for a while, then the Eldorado, and finally Rumors. Today the property is a parking lot.

Another venue that offered entertainment was the Terrace Room in the Statler Hotel. Opened in 1912, the hotel, at 1127 Euclid Avenue, was designed by George B. Post and boasted 700 guest rooms. It was considered the most elegant hotel in the Statler Chain, and it prided itself on the Statler philosophy that "the guest is always right." The hotel's capacity was soon increased to 1,000 rooms via an addition to the east.

The new facility for the exclusive Union Club opened to members in 1905. *(Richard Karberg collection)*

The main dining room of the Union Club was designed to create a comfortable yet masculine setting for lunch or dinner. *(Cleveland Press Collection of the Cleveland State University Archives)*

This is how the Cleveland Athletic Club appeared in a rendering by its architect, Milton Dyer.

(Richard Karberg collection)

The Statler had a men's dining room on the first floor (a space later occupied by a Marie Schreiber's Chop House and then a Swingos restaurant) and the balconied Pompeian Room on the mezzanine level, a dining space which Cleveland *Press* columnist Winsor French called the most "handsome restaurant in town." That space later was renamed the Terrace Room. Reached via a grand staircase from the two-story lobby, the high-ceilinged room was fitted into an interior courtyard. The original ceiling was later lowered, and the grand staircase disappeared after the Hilton Hotel chain bought the Statler properties in 1954 and extensively renovated the building. The Terrace Room

offered entertainment along with its fine dining. Many will remember the appearances of Nelson Eddy and the Sammy Watkins Orchestra. The Terrace Room closed in 1965, a victim of a growing preference for less formal dining and a decline in hotel occupancy.

The hotel was sold again in 1973 and renamed the Cleveland Plaza, with some floors being converted to office space. In 1980 the building was converted entirely to office use as the Statler Office Tower. In 2002, following extensive remodeling which restored some of the elegant details lost in earlier renovations, it was reincarnated as the Statler Arms Apartments.

The upper avenue was also home to several other eateries, some of which had fairly long life spans. The longest survivor among these was the Colonnade Cafeteria in the Bulkley Building (1931-1972), which during the 1950s frequently served lunch daily to 2,000 patrons. Other restaurants included the Playhouse Square Restaurant (1948-1965); the Gazelle Restaurant at 1132 Euclid (1948-1967); and the Black Angus at 1326 Huron Road, on the former site of the Hotel Euclid (1955-1975).

For many, however, dining on the upper avenue meant "the club." Upper Euclid Avenue was home to four of the city's best known private clubs, and each offered their members dining choices. Three of the four are still in existence.

The most exclusive of these, the Union Club, was established in 1872 as a gathering place for "men of influence." Since 1905 the club has occupied a handsome four-story renaissance-style building on Euclid Avenue at East 12th Street. The building was designed by noted Cleveland architect Charles Schweinfurth. A chief feature is the formal dining room on the third floor. The pillared and dark-paneled room offers members a venue not only for breakfast, lunch, or dinner, but also a place where "grand ideas" can be discussed in comfort. A second dining room, somewhat less formal in setting and tone, is located on the first floor. Another dining room on the third floor at one time was reserved for women guests. That was during an era when women were not allowed to enter through the front door and had to take their own elevator to the third floor. During the 1970s and 1980s the Union Club did away with restrictions to membership based on gender or ethnicity.

Another of the upper avenue clubs is the Cleveland Athletic Club (CAC), founded in 1908. Looking for a permanent home, the CAC arranged to build its headquarters over a five-story building then under construction at 1118 Euclid Avenue. Designed by J. Milton

Dyer, the terra cotta-faced building has been home to the CAC since 1911. In addition to a bowling alley, swimming pool, gymnasium, track, and other athletic facilities on the top floors (as well as 15 guest rooms), the club also provides several different locations for dining. A popular spot for a hamburger and a coke is the counter in Frank's Place on the 11th floor. Lunch and breakfast are served in the Regency Room on the seventh floor, and dinner is available in the elegant Tavern Room on the sixth floor. Meals can also be served in any of the five parlors which occupy the eighth floor. During the upper avenue's glory days, as many as 500 people were served lunch at the CAC daily.

The third club on the upper avenue was the Mid-Day Club, formed in 1924 as a businessmen's club and housed on the 21st floor of the Union Trust Building (Huntington Building). The penthouse floor was originally intended as a waiting room for passengers of a zeppelin service which

Lunch at the Cleveland Athletic Club was always an enjoyable event, with good food and excellent service—c. 1970. (Cleveland Press Collection of the Cleveland State University Archives)

The architecture of Rohr's Restaurant reflected a central European background—1936. (Cleveland Press Collection of the Cleveland State University Archives)

Ball Room, opened to the public for lunch. It is also available for private parties.

The Hermit Club, while not directly on Euclid Avenue, is just around the corner at 1639 Dodge Court. This location, just north of the Playhouse Square theaters, is convenient for members who share an interest in the performing arts. The club's Tudor-style building was designed by Cleveland architect Frank Meade in 1928. The Hermit Club offers it members quiet reading and social rooms as well as a lounge and dining rooms.

Some restaurants that appealed to the upper avenue crowd were located just off Euclid Avenue, only a short stroll away from the stores. Three favorite spots were to be found on Chester Avenue's restaurant row, between East Ninth and East Twelfth streets on the north side of Chester. These were particularly convenient to those working in the Union Trust (Huntington) Building.

Operated by Marie Schreiber, The Tavern Chop House, at 1027 Chester Avenue, was a popular lunch and dinner spot. Known for its generous drinks, delicious cuisine, and excellent service, the restaurant also had a distinctive atmosphere. The walls were covered with framed paintings and stuffed animal heads, and the booths were particularly comfortable. The Tavern Chop House survived until the site was claimed for an urban renewal project in 1967. Marie Schreiber then transferred her menu to the plush new dining room at the Hollenden House. Later she opened another Chop House at the Statler. The food in the new dining rooms faithfully replicated the traditional Schreiber favorites, but the new

would have connected Cleveland with Chicago and New York. Planners, however, did not take into account the strong wind gusts off Lake Erie which would have made landing an air ship there much too risky. Another use for the waiting room had to be found, and it became the main dining room for the Mid-Day Club. The room was the city's largest private dining space, capable of comfortably seating 400 guests, and affording them a wonderful view of downtown Cleveland. The club also sported a bar and eight smaller meeting/dining rooms. Suffering from a decline in membership, the Mid-Day Club folded in 1990, but the space was not long idle. In 1991 the spacious dining room, renamed Sammy's Metropolitan

Today's Special — Split of Haut Sauterne Wine 65c

SPECIAL FROM OUR CHARCOAL GRILL
PRIME BOSTON LOIN STEAK
WITH THIN SLICED RAW FRIED POTATOES
— $1.25 —
Dinner $1.75

Rohr's

SPECIAL SHORE DINNER
— $1.50 —
Steamed Soft Shell Clams
Whole Broiled
Chicken Lobster
JULIENNE POTATOES
COLE SLAW
DINNER DESSERT
COFFEE

SPECIAL DINNERS
Price of Entree Determines Cost of Dinner

●

Assorted Relishes
Fresh Vegetable Minestrone or Puree of Mongole or
Fruit Cocktail   Pineapple Juice   Filet of Herring
Tomato Juice   Fresh Shrimp Cocktail   Fresh Crabmeat Cocktail
(6) Oysters or Clams on Half Shell 25c Extra

●

Broiled Fresh Swordfish Steak Hoteliere 1.25
Fresh Mountain Trout Saute Belle Meuniere, Garnished 1.40
Broiled Kippered Herring, Drawn Butter 1.20
Broiled Boston Blue Mackerel, Lemon Butter Sauce 1.20
Jumbo Louisiana Frog Fried in Butter, Sauce Remoulade 1.50
Fried Fresh Frog Legs, Tartar Sauce 1.45
Fresh Yellow Perch Whole, Saute Meuniere 1.30
Baked Whole Stuffed Lobster a la Thermidore 1.50
Broiled Fresh Eastern Salmon Steak Hoteliere 1.30
Fresh Shrimp and Lobster a la Newburg in Casserole 1.40
Broiled Fresh Halibut Steak Maitre d' Hotel 1.30
Whole Yellow Pike, Meuniere Butter 1.40
Fresh Filet of Blue Pike Saute, Fine Herbes 1.20
Whole Broiled Live Lobster, Drawn Butter 1.20
Broiled Fresh Lake Erie Whitefish, Lemon Butter 1.45
Fresh Fried Scallops, Tartar Sauce 1.20
Whole Florida Pompano Saute Meuniere 1.60
Fried Filet of Genuine Sole, Ravigotte Sauce 1.20
Potted Sirloin of Beef a la Moissoneuse 1.20
Roast Loin of Pork, Dressing, Pan Gravy 1.20
Broiled Prime Sirloin or Tenderloin Steak 2.00
Roast Young Stuffed Ohio Turkey, Giblet Gravy,
Cranberry Sauce 1.50
Baked Sugar Cured Ham, Raisin Sauce 1.20
Broiled Veal Kidney on Toast with Fresh Mushrooms 1.25
Emince of Chicken a la King en Casserole, Toast 1.25
Roast Long Island Duckling, Dressing, Compote of Prunes 1.35
Roast U. S. Prime Steer Ribs of Beef au Jus 1.60
Broiled Spring Lamb Chops, Pineapple Glace 1.60
Broiled Pork Chops with Apple Sauce, Watercress 1.40
Half Spring Chicken Broiled with Crisp Bacon, Toast 1.50
Calf's Liver Saute in Butter with Bacon or Onions 1.40

●

Mashed, Candied Sweet or French Fried Potatoes
New Green Peas au Beurre, Baked Hubbard Squash
or Buttered Leaf Spinach

●

Health Salad

●

Apple, Red Raspberry or Cocoanut Custard Pie
Cheese or Apple Strudel   Chocolate Eclair
Fruit Pudding, Vanilla Sauce   Fruit Jello
Chocolate or Vanilla Ice Cream
Kraft American, Swiss Gruyere or Roquefort Cheese
Coffee, Tea or Milk

A 1939 menu from Rohr's reflected a wide variety of European cuisine. *(Cleveland* Press *Collection of the Cleveland State University Archives)*

The Black Angus restaurant was at the southwest corner of Euclid Avenue and East 14th Street. It later became the Rusty Scupper—1964. *(Cleveland* Press *Collection of the Cleveland State University Archives)*

rooms, attractive as they were, could not match the ambiance of the original.

To either side of the Tavern were the Hickory Grille (929 Chester) and Rohr's Restaurant (1111 Chester), two long-time dining spots with a loyal following of lunch and dinner regulars. Both restaurants had "atmosphere," and their bars served generous drinks.

Joseph Schulman was the first owner of Hickory Grille which opened in 1935. Business was brisk right from the start, and so in 1939 the restaurant was expanded to seat 185. Though remodeled at times over the years, Hickory Grille decor always favored walnut (not hickory) paneling and fixtures. In 1948 the restaurant passed into the hands of the Isador Weinberger family, and the property was totally remodeled in 1960. While the renovated room took on some Early American design features, walnut again predominated. Silver mosaics, bearing the HG signature in aluminum, were added. The entranceway led

to a reception area, and then to the bar, with the dining room to the rear. The Hickory Grille served traditional American fare in an atmosphere the Weinbergers called the "most elegant in the midwest."

Rohr's Restaurant began as Fischer-Rohr on East Ninth Street in 1911. When it moved to Chester Avenue in 1918, the Fischer name was dropped. The restaurant was rather eclectic in its appointments; elements of German culture competed with painted caricatures of prominent Clevelanders. It was not the decor, however, that drew Clevelanders to Rohr's, but rather its excellent seafood specialties. The oyster stew and Lake Erie whitefish were especially popular, and Cleveland *Press* columnist Winsor French claimed Rohr's lobster was the city's absolute best.

Both the Hickory Grille and Rohr's closed after New Year's Eve farewell parties in 1966. Their buildings were razed to make way for construction of the Investment Plaza complex.

Just around the corner from the Chester Restaurant Row on East Ninth Street was Kornman's, another popular restaurant operated by the Weinberger family. It occupied the spot that had earlier been home to Fischer-Rohr. Staying open until 1:00 a.m., Kornman's was especially popular with late night diners and was a haven for sports figures and newspaper reporters. Kornman's decor was unpretentious, with walls which were paneled on the lower half and with wainscoting and painted brick above. Meals were served on bare oak tables. Kornman's continued to do a good business until its site was claimed for construction of Central National Bank's headquarters building (now the McDonald Building).

Next to Kornman's was Pat Joyce's, which was also in the path of the bank building development. Operated by Iggy McIntyre, Pat Joyce's relocated to East Sixth Street and St. Clair Avenue, but Kornman's, like so many of the other fondly remembered restaurants on the upper avenue, closed permanently, leaving only memories.

Restaurants have an ephemeral life. They are popular for a time, and then as times and tastes change, they fade away. Only the clubs' dining facilities have operated uninterruptedly to the present time. But though the popular restaurants of the upper avenue's heyday are long gone, they are still fondly remembered. So much of what is meaningful in human relationships and discourse takes place in the context of dining. Those significant moments are inextricably tied to the settings where they took place. And that is why the restaurants of upper Euclid Avenue remain bright in the memories of three generations of Greater Clevelanders.

Kornman's provided both fine food and an atmosphere which built a continuing clientele. Many Clevelanders patronized the owner when he established a new restaurant in Las Vegas— 1953. *(Cleveland* Press *Collection of the Cleveland State University Archives)*

IV

THE THEATERS
ON THE
UPPER AVENUE

BETTE DAVIS,
CLARK GABLE,
CAROL LOMBARD,
&
TOMMY DORSEY

In 1921 the development of the Playhouse Square district was almost complete. Notice, however, that the Keith Building has not yet made its appearance.
(Bruce Young collection)

WHILE THE MULTIPLEX cinema, clustering several movie screens in one location, may seem a modern innovation, the concept of a central entertainment district has a solid history. The development of Playhouse Square attests to that fact. For a period of time, the seven tenths of a mile that constitutes upper and lower Euclid Avenue was home to eleven theaters offering an appealing variety of amusements. Seven theaters were located on the upper avenue, and four were on the lower avenue. Their offerings ranged from vaudeville to legitimate theater to the motion picture, the form which over time became predominant.

The seven theaters on the upper avenue formed what came to be known as Playhouse Square, a development which was the brainchild of Cleveland real estate magnate Joseph Laronge. He envisioned the district as a smart mix of new theaters interspersed with the fashionable shops which were already in place. The Playhouse Square district took shape between 1916 and 1922.

The Stillman Theatre, at 1111 Euclid Avenue, came first. It opened its doors to the public on September 29, 1916. The entrance to the theater was carved out of the western end of the Hotel Statler, and its design features represented ideas of both the Cleveland firm of Walker and Weeks and those of the hotel's architect, George B. Post and Sons. The theater's name came from its site; it was built on land that once had been the Stillman Witt homestead.

From its inception the Stillman was intended as a venue for motion pictures. Despite that intent, however, it was somehow built without either a projection booth or an organ loft, which in the days before the "talkies" was a serious omission, and engineers were called in to make the necessary corrections. Its first play bill featured E. H. Sothern in *The Chattel* with the H. L. Spitalny

An eastbound streetcar rumbles through Playhouse Square at dusk. The scene is from early 1952.
(Jim Spangler collection)

This forbidding view of Playhouse Square in winter 1950 makes the theaters appear dark and lifeless. To the contrary, however, they were full of splendor, and the magic of films made them even more attractive. The Lake/Esquire Theatre is seen in the background.
(Bruce Young collection)

Orchestra providing the music. Auditorium seating for the evening opener was 15 cents; reserved seats in the orchestra section were 50 cents, and loge seating cost 75 cents.

The theater, which accommodated 1,800, was designed with audience comfort in mind. There was a promenade area on the mezzanine level, and steps leading to the balcony had recessed lighting. Uniformed ushers carried flashlights to guide patrons to their seats in the auditorium. Other amenities included a women's lounge and a men's smoking room (men could also smoke in the box seats). Wall coverings were silk, and the

ornamental plaster work copied both Renaissance and Louis XVI design elements.

The Stillman philosophy was to "operate the house for the convenience of guests rather than the convenience of employees." The management promised patrons that it would never excuse "any pertness or impudence" from any employee.

Operated over the years as part of the Loew's chain, the Stillman garnered several distinctions. It was the Cleveland house for the first all-sound movie, Al Jolson's *The Jazz Singer*, and it was the first Cleveland movie theater to copy the New York practice of operating on an all-reserved-seat basis when it screened *Broadway Melody* in 1929. It was also the local screen for the 1939-1940 blockbuster *Gone with the Wind*.

The Stillman's last day came on July 30, 1963, following an exclusive reserved-seat run of *Lawrence of Arabia*. By then attendance at the downtown movie theaters was declining. They were competing with suburban theaters in neighborhood shopping centers and malls, which had the advantage of being closer to home and offering free parking. With attendance revenue down and a property buyer at hand (the next door hotel needed parking), the end came. The theater's auditorium was demolished and replaced with a parking garage offering access directly to the neighboring Statler Hilton lobby. Today all that remains of the Stillman is the tracing of the old outer lobby's ornamental plaster adorning the top of the entry ramp leading into the garage—that and memories.

The State Theatre, at 1519 Euclid Avenue, and the Ohio Theatre, at 1511 Euclid Avenue, were built at the same time, the Ohio just to

The Stillman Theatre was elegant and convenient, yet it was the first of the grand theaters to be demolished. It was the venue for block-buster films as the line of these waiting to get in to see *Gone With the Wind* indicates. *(Cleveland* Press *Collection of the Cleveland State University Archives)*

The interior of the Stillman reflected the classical design used in many of the grand movie theaters. *(Cleveland* Press *Collection of the Cleveland State University Archives)*

Even during its demolition, the Stillman house showed off its magnificence. *(Cleveland* Press *Collection of the Cleveland State University Archives)*

In1956 the State and Ohio theaters were still major destinations for Cleveland moviegoers. *(Cleveland* Press *Collection of the Cleveland State University Archives)*

the west of the State. The two theaters were designed by Thomas W. Lamb, a noted theater architect, to fit the site: a narrow Euclid Avenue frontage and a more spacious footprint to the rear of the property which reaches to Dodge Court. Long lobbies stretch from the Euclid Avenue entrances to reach the auditoriums, which are situated side by side at the rear of the property. Both are embellished with lavish Italian Renaissance appointments.

The State Theatre, with 3,400 seats, was designed primarily as a movie house. It was said to have the longest lobby in the world. Lamb estimated that the lobby could accommodate 4,000 people. Totaling 180 feet in length, richly carpeted, lined with Corinthian columns, and topped by an ornate coffered ceiling, the lobby also featured four large murals by James Daugherty which depicted favorite themes of the entertainment industry.

The State opened on February 5, 1921, with the film *Polly with a Past* and the H. L. Spitalny Orchestra in the pit to provide the music. The State was operated as part of the Loew's theater chain, and the opening night festivities were attended by impresario Marcus Loew as well as a bevy of Hollywood stars.

Unlike the State, the Ohio was intended for stage productions, and its seating capacity was only 1,400. The Ohio opened on February 12, 1921, featuring David Warfield in *The Return of Peter Grimm*. It began operations as an independent house, but in 1922 it joined the State as part of the Loew's group.

Over the years the Ohio Theatre did not fare as well as the State. Dropped by the Loew's chain, the theater was in need of a new direction. In 1935 it was remodeled in art deco style and resurfaced as the Mayfair Casino nightclub. It was a risky venture in the Depression days, and the venture ended

Inside the State Theatre grand staircases, acres of carpeting, and large murals awaited the moviegoer, who felt he or she had arrived in a wonderland. Happily this entire splendor is intact today. *(Cleveland* Press *Collection of the Cleveland State University Archives)*

By the late 1960s both the State and Ohio were in financial trouble. Relatively few people were coming downtown to see movies, and as box office revenues dwindled, the costs of maintaining the gigantic movie palaces became prohibitive. The last day for both theaters came on February 9, 1969. The Ohio's last film was *Star*, and the State's was *Ice Station Zebra*. When the theaters closed that night, it appeared that their useful years had come to an end.

Things looked even more bleak three years later. In March 1972 the property's owners applied to the city for a demolition permit so that they could raze the theaters and replace them with a large parking lot. Thanks to the vision and determination of Ray Shepherdson, a campaign to save the theaters was launched. The lobby and the auditorium of the State Theatre became the base for ascertaining the future potential of the Playhouse Square district.

The crusade to save the theaters was lengthy, and the costs involved were

in bankruptcy in 1936. In the 1950s, however, the Ohio rebounded as a reserved-seat house, playing such Hollywood blockbusters as *The Ten Commandments*. Then in 1961 a serious fire resulted in a cheap remodeling that obscured much of the rich detail the theater had once known. By its last years, the Ohio's one-time glamor had faded.

The lobby of the Ohio Theatre was, if possible, even more glamorous than that of the State. *(Courtesy Playhouse Square Association, used by permission, Theatre Historical Society of America, Elmhurst, Illinois)*

The auditorium of the Ohio Theatre was extensively damaged by a fire in the early 1960s. It is now fully restored. *(Courtesy Playhouse Square Association, used by permission, Theatre Historical Society of America, Elmhurst, Illinois)*

significant. The struggle, however, ended in triumph. The State and its four neighboring theaters were not only saved from destruction, but completely restored to their former glory. They are now once again flourishing and drawing large crowds to the district (see *Playhouse Square: An Entertaining History* for more about the restoration effort).

The Allen Theatre, built for Jules and Jay Allen at 1501 Euclid Avenue, forms part of the Bulkley Building. Designed by C. Howard Crane, the development included an enclosed garage at the rear of the site, a consideration that was uncommon at the time. Built as a venue for movies, the Allen Theatre opened on April 1, 1921, with a double feature, *The Greatest Love* and *The Hallroom Boys*.

The Allen featured a shorter lobby than its neighbors to the east, and it ended in a two-story domed Italian Renaissance rotunda, 33 feet in height. Encircled by Corinthian columns and with balconies on the upper

level, the rotunda formed the entryway to the 3,400-seat auditorium. Interesting features of the elegant auditorium were its backlighted imitation windows and the oval opening over the rear seats which served as the center point of the balcony level foyer.

Over the years Allen management changed several times. Loew's ran the house from 1922 until 1932 when RKO took over, first alone and then in conjunction with Warner Brothers. The theater was under Stanley-Warner control from 1949 until its closing in 1968.

The Allen, like its neighbors on the upper avenue, began to struggle in the 1960s, and following a run with *Bonnie and Clyde*, it closed its doors on May 7, 1968.

The Allen became the first of the Playhouse Square theaters used in the campaign to save the theaters when it hosted the Budapest Symphony Orchestra in 1971. Over the next years, the Allen briefly housed a restaurant and a laserium theater,

By 1964 Playhouse Square theaters were presenting stage shows of British rock stars such as Peter and Gordon who performed at the Allen July 10, 1964. *(Cleveland* Press *Collection of the Cleveland State University Archives)*

and it became the fourth of district theaters to be fully restored.

The Hanna Theatre occupied a somewhat different niche from the other theaters that were finding a home on Playhouse Square. It was built as a legitimate theater to replace the aging Euclid Avenue Opera House, which was owned by the Hanna family. Located on Euclid Avenue at East 4th Street, the Opera House had been the city's most important stage since 1875. When the Hanna Theatre opened, the Euclid Avenue Opera House was no longer needed. It closed in 1922.

The Hanna Theatre opened on March 28, 1921, with a production of Mark Twain's *The Prince and the Pauper.* The theater was named in honor of Marcus Alonzo Hanna, founder of the Hanna business empire, a leader in the national Republican Party, and one of Ohio's U.S. senators.

Fitted into the eight-story annex of the 16-story Hanna Building, the theater's front

doors face East 14th Street, between Prospect and Euclid avenues. Charles A. Platt, architect for the project, designed the complex in the Italian Renaissance style. Travertine marble was predominant in the lobby and corridor areas. The theater auditorium, seating 1,535, was richly ornamented in the Pompeian style, its decorative motif featuring a series of classical figures. Etched across the sounding board was a list of the greatest dramatists of all time, a feature that often drew puzzled looks from theater-goers who were not familiar with the icons of stage history. One frequently cited drawback to the theater was its lack of generous lobby space, a characteristic in marked contrast with the other theaters in the district. Shoulder rubbing prior to opening act or during intermissions proved more than a cliche when the Hanna had a full house.

Over the years the Hanna Theatre typically featured Broadway productions which came to Cleveland either after their run in

New York had ended, or sometimes as part of the preparation for their New York debut. Hanna productions were originally tied into the Shubert Circuit and then later into the United Booking network. While Cleveland had other legitimate theaters (Cleveland Play House foremost among them, with Cleveland's Music Hall the stage for some touring productions), it was to the Hanna that Clevelanders typically turned for the Broadway-style show. Ably led by manager Milton Krantz for 42 years (1941-1983), the theater succeeded in hosting the most celebrated stage productions of the day. A sampling of the shows that played the Hanna stage includes such classics as *Lysistrata* and *Hamlet*, musicals like *Oklahoma* and *South Pacific*, and such 1970s-style shows as *Hair* and *No, No, Nanette*. The Hanna also had the distinction of hosting the premiere of the Rodgers and Hammerstein show *Me and Juliette*.

While the other theaters in Playhouse Square closed during the 1960s, the Hanna soldiered on alone, keeping the lights of the Square from being totally extinguished. In 1966, in fact, Hanna management invested in a new orchestra pit and sound system as well as for an adjacent parking garage for theater patrons. In 1971 stage lighting was improved, and the marquee was refurbished. Of all the Playhouse Square theaters, the Hanna proved the most durable. In the Hanna's first 50 years of operation (1921-1971), approximately six million patrons attended its hundreds of productions, a testament to both the appealing venue and the well-chosen attractions.

As lavish as the other theaters on Playhouse Square were, the Palace Theatre has to be ranked at the top of the list. Its name accurately depicts its elegance. Built to the specifications of Edward Albee and forming part of the 21-story B. F. Keith Building (then the tallest building in the city), the theater was meant to serve as the Cleveland home for the

The rotunda of the lobby area in the Allen Theatre was one of the most sophisticated architectural features of all of the theater lobbies at Playhouse Square. *(Cleveland* Press *Collection of the Cleveland State University Archives)*

The distinctive marquee of the Hanna Theatre suggested the refined architecture of the theatre and its intimate lobby. (*Cleveland* Press *Collection of the Cleveland State University Archives*)

This souvenir program is from March 28, 1921, the opening night of the Hanna Theatre. (*Cleveland* Press *Collection of the Cleveland State University Archives*)

Keith vaudeville circuit. Designed by the Chicago firm of Rapp and Rapp, the Palace opened on November 6, 1922. The theater owners proudly claimed that the Palace was the "most beautiful playhouse in the world." Featuring a liberal use of marble, the most stunning feature of the theater was its inner three-story lobby with its graceful marble staircases leading to the balcony level. The upper promenade was graced with tapestries and gilt-framed oil paintings. The splendidly detailed auditorium could seat 3,680. An extensive backstage area provided excellent accommodations for the performers.

In its first years, the Palace served exclusively as a vaudeville house, and a veritable who's who of show business performed on its stage. Opening night featured Elsie Janis, Grace Hayes, and the Cansinos, along with an assortment of warm-up acts. In 1926 the Palace added movies to its bill of fare, but stage shows continued to be a major component of its presentations. As vaudeville faded, however, movies became the theater's main fare, and in its last years, bulky projection booths were built onto the main floor so that Cinerama features could be projected onto a newly installed curved screen. The theater's last feature was the Cinerama production, *Krakatoa, East of Java*. The end finally came on July 20, 1969. And as the lights in the Palace marquee were turned off for the last time, the movie era on Playhouse Square came to an end.

Today, like its neighbors to the west, the Palace has been faithfully restored so that little of its splendor has been lost. Each August the restored Palace holds an abbreviated film season as a reminder of the theater's wonderful past as a movie house.

The Lake Theatre, the last theater to open on the upper avenue, is probably the least remembered of the seven. Situated at 1630 Euclid Avenue, immediately east of the Alpine Village supper club, the Lake opened in 1928. The "Lake" was actually not the theater's original name; it had three names during its relatively brief presence (1928-1951) on the avenue. In 1928 it opened as the Cinema Theatre, but then in 1930, when it became a part of the Stanley Warner chain, its name was changed to the Lake Theatre, the name it kept the longest. During its last three years, 1948-1951, it operated under the Community Circuit Theaters umbrella and was known as the Esquire Theater.

The Lake was neither as large nor as lavish as its neighbors on the north side of the avenue. It was built to seat 760, but that number was later reduced to 700 to provide more leg room for patrons.

During its years of service, the Lake had several periods when it went dark and its management sought to devise the best strategy for filling the seats. It started as a

The inner lobby of the Palace Theatre probably gave the theater goer a thrill akin to arriving in a genuine royal palace. Brocade-lined walls covered with oil paintings provided the sumptuous setting appropriate for a journey into a land of magic and wonderment.
(Cleveland Press *Collection of the Cleveland State University Archives)*

The Lake Theater (left) was
the only one of the Playhouse
Square theaters on the
south side of Euclid Avenue.
The Palace and the State
theaters are to the right.
(Cleveland Press *Collection
of the Cleveland State
University Archives)*

single-run house, but then shifted to a dou-ble-feature format in 1939, the only upper avenue theater to try this approach. After another shutdown period, the theater was extensively remodeled and reopened in 1942. In 1948 it closed again, and management passed from the Warner chain to the Community Circuit chain. Following further renovations, the Lake reopened as the Esquire, and the single-feature format was again adopted.

As the Esquire, the theater had one brief period of success, that coming when the feature *Red Shoes* was held over for an 18-week run. By 1951, however, attendance had dropped significantly, a situation which the-ater management attributed to the inroads that television was making on the movie audience. The theater's last day come on May 28, 1951.

The building was not vacant for long, however. The space was renovated, given a new Early American exterior, and became the home of television station WXEL, Channel 9 (which later became WJW, Channel 8). Perhaps the Esquire people were correct, at least in this one instance: television had come to supersede the motion picture. The building which housed both the theater and the television studios was torn down after WJW (then WJKW) moved to its new headquarters on the lakefront in 1975.

Of the seven theaters that once were a part of Playhouse Square, the five grandest remain. Thanks to the leadership of the Playhouse Square Foundation and its predecessor organizations, as well as to the generous support of foundations, government agencies, and many individuals, the district is once again alive, and its glorious architectural and cultural heritage preserved. Nowadays, one million theater goers each year give thanks.

Banners with the portrait of presidential candidate Wendell Wilkie hung over Euclid Avenue at Playhouse Square during the presidential election of 1940, adding to the area's sense of liveliness. (Cleveland Press Collection of the Cleveland State University Archives)

V

THE LOWER AVENUE

DOUBLE EAGLE STAMPS & DIME STORE COKES

LIKE THE UPPER AVENUE, lower Euclid Avenue, stretching from Public Square to East Ninth Street, was anchored by four well-known landmarks. At its western end, where Euclid funnels into Public Square, were the May Company and the Williamson Building. The May Company Building, with its familiar eight-story terra cotta facade, was designed by Daniel Burnham and Company of Chicago, and opened in October 1915. Across the street stood the 16-story Williamson Building, designed by George B. Post and Sons. When it opened in 1900, the Williamson Building, was the city's tallest structure.

At the southwestern corner of Euclid Avenue and East Ninth Street stood the 14-story Schofield Building (now the Euclid-Ninth Tower). Built by Levi Scofield (CQ), the designer of the Soldiers and Sailors Monument on Public Square, the building opened in 1902.

While these three anchors of the lower avenue were fixed during the described era, the northwestern corner experienced a dramatic change. The eight-story Hickox

commercial block, with its famous clock tower, occupied the site from 1890 until 1946. Then in 1946, the Columbus-based Bond Stores took over the site and hired Cleveland's Walker and Weeks and Chicago's Herbert Beidler to design a three-story showroom. The result was one of the very few buildings in Cleveland in the modernistic style. Its striking features, both exterior and interior, were in marked contrast to the traditional structures that lined Euclid Avenue. The new Bond store opened in 1947.

Between the anchors, the lower avenue was packed with stores, eating places, and theaters. What the lower avenue lacked in panache, it made up for in commercial activity. Cleveland had a burgeoning working class population who were quite bargain conscious. Though of modest means, they were still interested in style, and they found it on the lower avenue. The volume of shoppers, attracted by the more reasonable prices

Even before the time when Euclid Avenue was the "Sophisticated Lady," the street was bustling as the heart of the office and shopping district. At the right is the Hickox Building, one of the city's early prominent business blocks. (Cleveland Press Collection of the Cleveland State University Archives)

The May Company Building was a distinctive piece of architecture reminiscent of the work which its architect Daniel Burnham and Sons had done in designing the Wrigley Building in Chicago. *(Cleveland* Press *Collection of the Cleveland State University Archives)*

The Bond clothing store, designed in 1946 by the Cleveland firm of Walker and Weeks, was downtown Cleveland's only truly futuristic structure. *(Cleveland Press photo, Jim Toman collection)*

of merchandise in the stores there, made for crowded sidewalks and busy cash registers. The lower avenue had "bustle."

Department stores developed in three categories, small, medium, and large. Today it is hard to imagine that cities would have several stores in each of these categories, but Cleveland, like other U.S. and European cities, did provide consumers with an array of stores as well as of merchandise. On the lower avenue Cleveland shoppers had both a large- and a medium-sized store to choose from.

Among the city's department stores, William Taylor and Son was in the mid-range in size as well as in its price structure. Founded in 1870 and located in the

A men's hat box from Bond's—c. 1950. *(Courtesy of Paulette's Vintage)*

Taylor department store ladies' hat box from the 1950s. *(Courtesy of Paulette's vintage)*

This view of Bond's second and third floors gives an idea of the dramatic sense of space conveyed by the modernistic design. *(Western Reserve Historical Society)*

Taylor's main floor went through several remodelings and by 1958 had an austere neo-classical quality. *(Cleveland* Press *Collection of the Cleveland State University Archives)*

Cushing block on Public Square, the firm eventually outgrew that space. By 1907 it had moved to a new building, designed by Lehman and Schmidt, on Euclid Avenue at East Sixth Street. Taylor's soon outgrew its new space, and in 1914 four additional floors were added. The building received another addition in 1923.

A unique feature of the Taylor store was its Arcade located at the easterly end of the main building along Prospect Avenue. The Arcade was lined with many smaller shops, and the setting created a feeling of being in a store within a store.

Taylor's offered the full range of merchandise one expected to find in a modern department store. Its nine floors offered clothing, domestics, china, toys, household items, and furniture. Taylor's budget basement store was particularly popular. The basement was also the site of a small tea room.

For many years the store was managed by Sophie Strong. In support of her conservative values the Taylor store followed a policy of drawing black drapes across its Euclid Avenue display windows to prohibit window shopping on Sundays.

In 1934, in the midst of the great Depression, Taylor's undertook an extensive remodeling program in order to make it more competitive with the larger department stores. Three years earlier Higbee's had moved into its large new store on Public Square, May Company had added three floors, and Halle Bros. had remodeled its interior. At the time of its remodeling, Taylor's received congratulatory cablegrams

from the heads of Selfridge's and Harrod's in London. These cablegrams acknowledged the distinction of the remodeled Taylor store and included Taylor's in an international league of stores, of which the British, of course, were the recognized leaders.

In 1939 May Company (the parent firm of the Cleveland store) acquired a majority interest in Taylor's. This acquisition was kept secret until 1945 when another remodeling took place, made possible only by the vast financial resources of the national firm.

In 1958 Taylor's followed the pattern of other Cleveland department stores and opened a suburban branch store in the Southgate shopping center. At the same time, it opened a parking garage on Prospect Avenue, hoping that its presence would bolster patron use of the downtown store. But with sales slipping, the May Company parent firm decided to consolidate its Cleveland operations. It closed the Euclid Avenue Taylor store on December 16, 1961, and converted the Southgate branch to a May Company outlet. The upper floors of the Euclid Avenue

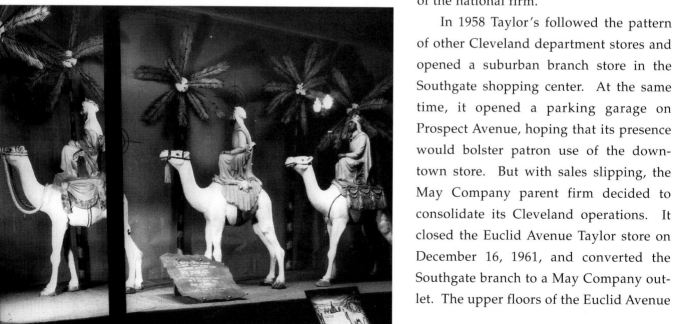

Even at the end of its days Taylor's elevator lobby and other features of the store reflected the traditions of department store architecture—1961. *(Cleveland* Press *Collection of the Cleveland State University Archives)*

During the Second World War Taylor's prided itself on stocking British merchandise which was typically considered the most desirable. *(Taylor's advertisement, Richard Karberg collection)*

property were later converted to office space. The street level was maintained as retail space.

The large department store on the lower avenue belonged to The May Company. In 1899 David May bought the E. R. Hull & Dutton Company store on Ontario Street, and introduced Clevelanders to The May Company. May's motto was "Watch Us Grow," and the company aggressively pursued plans to have a Euclid Avenue frontage. It began to buy properties facing the Square at Euclid Avenue's western edge. In 1902, May Company opened a six-story annex in remodeled space facing Public Square. When Taylor's moved farther east on the avenue, May's bought its former headquarters as well as some neighboring buildings as the site for its permanent new home. By 1912 May's controlled all the property it needed. The site was cleared, and construction began.

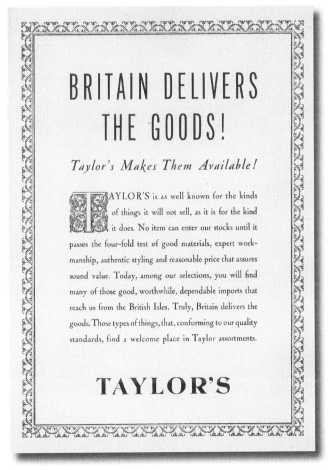

BRITAIN DELIVERS THE GOODS!

Taylor's Makes Them Available!

TAYLOR'S is as well known for the kinds of things it will not sell, as it is for the kind it does. No item can enter our stocks until it passes the four-fold test of good materials, expert workmanship, authentic styling and reasonable price that assures sound value. Today, among our selections, you will find many of those good, worthwhile, dependable imports that reach us from the British Isles. Truly, Britain delivers the goods. Those types of things, that, conforming to our quality standards, find a welcome place in Taylor assortments.

TAYLOR'S

May Company was a national department store company which furnished such items as its 1930 May Company Cook Book to its entire chain. *(Richard Karberg collection)*

The May Company basement was famous for its bargains. Here shoppers are buying Christmas cards at half price on December 26, 1963. *(Cleveland* Press *Collection of the Cleveland State University Archives)*

The May Company displayed a large array of merchandise across its selling floors, including its third floor millinery department—1931. *(Cleveland* Press *Collection of the Cleveland State University Archives)*

Designed by Daniel Burnham and Company of Chicago, the new building was five stories tall and stretched from Euclid Avenue to Prospect Avenue, giving May's one million square feet of space. It was the nation's most modern department store and the largest in Ohio. The store had 23 elevators and four sets of escalators, the first in Cleveland. The new building also offered a children's playroom and an auditorium for lectures and musical entertainments. The

May Company officially opened its new building on Monday, October 18, 1915.

Like its competitors on the avenue during the downtown shopping heyday, May's soon outgrew its space. Company management turned to architects Graham, Anderson, Probst, and White of Chicago, the successor to Burnham's firm, for a solution to the problem. The answer was a three-story addition atop its existing five-story main building. The new space opened in 1931.

While The May Company was downtown's largest store, it featured mid-range prices and offered shoppers an additional inducement by issuing trading stamps for purchases which could later be redeemed for store merchandise. Its huge bargain basement was another attraction. The combination of a wide range of competitively priced merchandise and the store's location at Public Square, the city's public transportation hub, made May's a winner with Cleveland shoppers. The downtown store outlasted all but one of the other downtown department stores, not closing until January 31, 1992. Although the store was

still showing a profit, it no longer fit into the suburban-oriented merchandising model preferred by the chain's corporate officers in St. Louis. When the downtown store closed, its suburban branch stores were renamed as part of the Kaufman division of The May Company chain.

By the early twentieth century the variety store, often called the five and dime or simply the dime store, had captured the imagination of the American public. These stores offered a wide array of merchandise displayed in beguiling ways and offered at low prices. They were found on both the upper and lower sections of Euclid Avenue. A number of the national dime store chains had stores in Cleveland, but the four which are most remembered are the F. W. Woolworth Company, the S. S. Kresge Company, the W. T. Grant Company, and McCrory's. All had stores on or near Euclid Avenue, and some had more than one location on Cleveland's main street.

From 1904 until 1950, Woolworth's had a store on East 4th Street, just off Euclid Avenue, but in 1950 it replaced that store with a new one at 330-340 Euclid Avenue, on the site of the former Central National Bank building. The former bank building had been demolished and in just twelve months replaced by a three-story building in the art

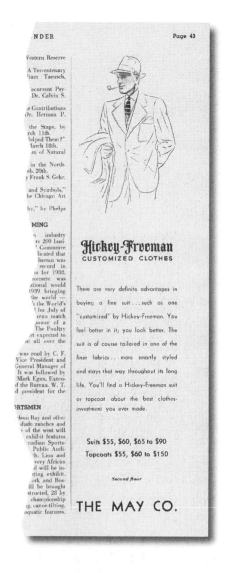

The May Company did not take a back seat in terms of high fashion as this advertisement for the British War Relief Ball program, held in Cleveland December 28, 1940, illustrates.
(Richard Karberg collection)

The May Company did not forget men and carried high quality men's suits—1938.
(May Company advertisement, Richard Karberg collection)

moderne style. It was designed by Garfield, Harris, Robinson and Schaefer, who also designed the Woodhill Homes project. The new store offered two levels of selling space and an 157-seat lunch counter. Upper floors included offices, an employee cafeteria, a bakery, a kitchen, and storage areas.

For many years Kresge's maintained two stores on Euclid Avenue. One location was at East 4th and Euclid (402 Euclid) in a building designed in 1922 by Walker and Weeks. The building contained two floors of selling space, a lunch counter, and two floors for

offices and storage. The second Kresge store was located at the eastern end of the May Company Building at 216 Euclid Avenue, just off Public Square. The store had no direct connection to The May Company, but like the May's store, it extended from Euclid Avenue through to Prospect Avenue. Refreshment counters stood at both ends of the store, with a sit-down lunch counter situated in the center of the store. The store opened when the May Company building was completed and remained in business until the late 1980s.

W. T. Grant was located at 240 Euclid Avenue in buildings designed by Starrett and Van Vleck and Alfred Altschuler for the former Chandler store and the former Ames Department Store, which opened early in the twentieth century and closed during the Depression. Grant's opened on the site in 1939 and remained in business there until the mid 1970s.

McCrory's, the other major dime store in downtown Cleveland, was located on East 4th Street between Euclid and Prospect avenues.

There were several clothing stores located along the lower avenue. Richman Brothers, a name familiar to most Clevelanders, entered the downtown retail business in 1903. The company had begun as a men's clothing manufacturer and later operated a huge clothing factory on East 55th Street. Richman's first retail store at Prospect Avenue and Ontario Street was

The famous Eagle Stamp books were a prominent feature of May Company marketing strategy. *(Richard Karberg collection)*

soon followed by a second store at 725 Euclid Avenue. That location was replaced in 1939 by a large new store on the south side of the avenue, between the Citizens and Hippodrome buildings at 736 Euclid. Moderately priced men's wear and its home-town appeal made Richman's a popular stop. By 1968 Richman Brothers had

F. W. Woolworth and W. T. Grant were adjacent to each other on Euclid Avenue and were neck to neck in the competitive market of dime store sales. *(Cleveland* Press *Collection of the Cleveland State University Archives)*

A tremendous array of
merchandise attracted the
eyes of Woolworth shoppers
on the spacious main floor
of its store at 330 Euclid
Avenue. *(Cleveland* Press
*Collection of the Cleveland
State University Archives)*

The lunch counter was a
prominent feature at the East
4th Street Woolworth's—
c. 1940. *(Cleveland* Press
*Collection of the Cleveland
State University Archives)*

Waitresses await the lunch crowd at W. T. Grant's counter. This photo was taken in 1940 shortly after the store's opening. (*Cleveland* Press *Collection of the Cleveland State University Archives*)

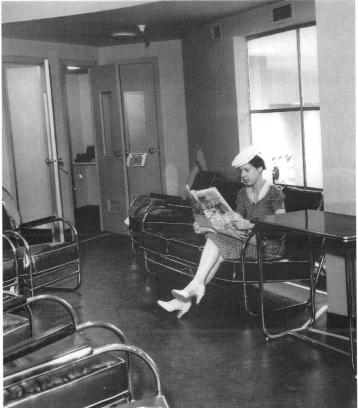

The W. T. Grant store had a women's lounge, an amenity unusual in the typical variety store—c. 1940. (*Cleveland* Press *Collection of the Cleveland State University Archives*)

Woolworth's was well known for the value of its own private label merchandise. (*Richard Karberg collection*)

77

Richman Bros.'s was first located on the north side of Euclid Avenue. The firm had several retail locations, as well as its head offices and manufacturing plant, in Cleveland. *(Cleveland Press Collection of the Cleveland State University Archives)*

Richman Bros. hat box— c. 1950. *(Courtesy of Paulette's Vintage)*

become the nation's largest manufacturer of men's clothing, an achievement that made it an acquisition target by other retail companies. In 1968 the F. W. Woolworth Company of New York made a bid for the Richman stores which was too attractive to pass up. The company was then managed as a Woolworth subsidiary, but it continued to operate under the Richman name. In 1969 Richman's remodeled its Euclid Avenue store, and its former rather nondescript interior was changed to resemble a private club for men of means. The Richman Brothers chain survived until 1992, when its parent company decided to close down the operation.

The Bond Company moved to Euclid Avenue in 1916, occupying space in the Hickox Block at East Ninth Street, before moving into its new building in 1947 (since razed to make way for the National City Center project). Bond's sold clothing for the whole family, although its men's wear department was predominant.

Rosenblum's was another clothier whose advertising jingle is still remembered by some: "One, you go to Rosenblum's to clothe the family; two, you name your budget terms, no extras no sirree; three, you turn the numbers round, and this is what you see— Rosenblum's 321 Euclid."

Rosenblum's started in business in 1910 on Ontario Street, moving to its Euclid Avenue address in 1919 (where the BP Tower now stands). What made Rosenblum's particularly appealing to families of modest means was that it offered customers extended credit plans, and nearly two thirds of its customers took advantage of these terms.

And there was much more on the lower avenue to attract shoppers. The grand Arcade (it needed no other descriptor), designed by John Eisenmann and George Smith, opened in 1890. The Arcade may be thought of as the 19th Century predecessor of the shopping mall. Extending between Euclid Avenue and Superior Avenue, its five-story central length was lined with shops and offices.

The lower avenue also had two smaller arcades, stretching between Euclid Avenue and Prospect Avenue. The Colonial Arcade (1898) and the Euclid Arcade (1892), both two stories high, were also designed by George Smith. All three arcades were lined with small shops, offering passers-by everything from hair cuts to shoe repair, stamps and coins, jewelry and curios, cards and gifts, luncheonettes, and a whole lot more.

Many of these smaller stores developed a loyal clientele, much as had Record Rendezvous on Prospect Avenue. It became

Cleveland's Arcade, with its rich architectural detail, has been a major Cleveland landmark since 1890. *(Richard Karberg photo)*

The Colonial Arcade in the 1960s used its center passageway to good advantage as the site for an automotive exhibition. *(Cleveland Press Collection of the Cleveland State University Archives)*

a leader by carrying rock and roll and rhythm and blues albums, often on obscure labels and by yet-unknown artists. Among the smaller stores lining the lower avenue were: Burrows Bros. stationers; I. J. Fox furs; the Lerner, Three Sisters, and K. & B. clothing stores; the Danford & Lowell, Green's, and Rotbart's jewelry stores; the Majestic Tie Shop; the Busch, Cole, and Thom McCan shoe stores; the Gray, Standard, and Marshall drug stores; and for a time even an S & H trading stamp redemption center. The stores on lower Euclid had something for everyone.

Interspersed among the shops and stores was an assortment of dining spots. Besides the Clark's and Stouffer's restaurants (described earlier), the lunchrooms in May's and Taylor's, and the lunch counters in the

Lower Euclid Avenue was the home to many shops, restaurants, and other commercial establishments. *(Cleveland Transit System Photo, Jim Toman collection)*

dime stores, there were several other independent eateries on the lower avenue.

Cafeterias were particularly popular. One of the most enduring was the Mills Restaurant at 315 Euclid Avenue. Mills opened for business in 1919, one of the first downtown cafeteria-style eateries. Its prime rib and fried chicken were its most popular entrees, while strawberry shortcake headed its dessert list. Mills was remodeled in 1930 and again in 1948. The restaurant survived until 1971.

Another eatery was the Russet Cafeteria. It opened for business in 1932 on the lower level of the Hippodrome Building at 780 Euclid Avenue, but in 1946 moved to larger quarters in the Citizens Building (now the City Club Building) at 850 Euclid Avenue. There was also another Russet Cafeteria on the upper avenue, just east of the Halle Bros. store.

The Pickwick Cafeteria, originally in the Arcade, moved to lower Superior Avenue, and then in 1956 moved to 643 Euclid Avenue, across from the Taylor store, in a building that had earlier hosted the Blue Boar Restaurant.

Another cafeteria, just south of Euclid Avenue on East Ninth Street, was the Forum Cafeteria, which opened on the first floor of the Rose Building in 1931. A popular feature was its two serving lines, which enabled harried lunch goers to spend more time at their table and less going through the line. In 1964 the Forum was renovated, and a take-out service was added. The "fast food" craze was making inroads in the more traditional dining habits that had predominated downtown.

For those who liked Chinese food, a popular spot was the Nanking Restaurant on the lower level of the Hippodrome Building, in the space earlier occupied by the Russet Cafeteria. The Nanking moved to the Hippodrome from a site on Huron Road. With a seating capacity of 500, the Nanking was the city's largest Chinese restaurant.

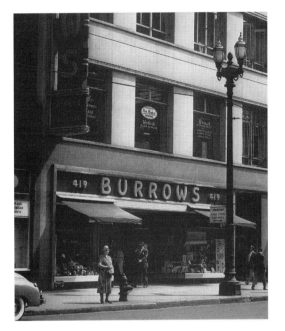

Burrows Brothers was a famous Cleveland-based stationery, book, and office supply business. For many years it had a store located at 419 Euclid, just east of the Arcade—1949. *(Cleveland* Press *Collection of the Cleveland State University Archives)*

While not located on Euclid Avenue, the Forum was the most legendary of the many downtown cafeterias and drew patrons from the entire downtown area. *(Cleveland* Press *Collection of the Cleveland State University Archives)*

Nanking at the Hipp opened in 1946 and
continued in business until 1962.

The lower avenue also had its share of
theaters. After the Euclid Avenue Opera
House closed in 1922, the Hippodrome
Theater became the avenue's oldest entertainment palace. Located at 720 Euclid
Avenue, it was designed by the Boston part-
nership of Knox and Elliot and opened on

January 2, 1908. The Hipp's seating capacity
was 4,100, and the B. F. Keith Circuit,
which booked the vaudeville acts that
appeared there, claimed that the Cleveland
Hippodrome was the second largest theater
in the world.

The theater, part of the Hippodrome
Building, was sandwiched between office
towers on Euclid Avenue and on Prospect
Avenue, and had entrances on both avenues.
The two outer lobbies joined in a central lobby
(total lobby length 412 feet), which was sup-
ported by massive pillars with Egyptian-
motif capitals. From the central lobby a grand
staircase led to the balcony levels. Variety
reported that the Hippodrome had the "hand-
somest proscenium arch in the country," and
that the acoustics were "nearly perfect."

The opening production featured two
spectaculars, *Coaching* and *The Cloudburst,*

with interesting theatrical effects that the theater's large stage and backstage area could easily support. The opening night also featured a series of vaudeville acts, including the Sharp Brothers, Mabel Berra, and the Musical Avolas.

Over the years, the Hippodrome operated under a number of management arrangements. It started as an independent house, then was carried as part of the B. F. Keith, R.K.O., and Stanley Warner syndicates, before ending its career once again as an independent. The Hippodrome hosted a broad spectrum of entertainments, including opera with Enrico Caruso, symphonic fare under the baton of Arturo Toscanini, and plays starring the famous Sarah Bernhardt and Ethyl Barrymore.

As time passed and the motion picture became the entertainment rage, it was necessary for the Hipp to make structural changes dictated by the projection screen. And so in 1931, although the backstage dressing rooms disappeared, the pitch of the balconies was altered, and the boxes were removed, the house continued to boast 4,000 seats. From then to its closing in 1980, the Hippodrome was primarily a movie house. It typically played first-run films and attracted good crowds, such as when it premiered the first 3-D movie, the sci-fi thriller *It Came from Outer Space* in 1953. It had the distinction of surviving as a movie theater longer than any of the other Euclid Avenue theaters, but its time too eventually ran out. The last day came on May 2, 1980, with the screening of *Drums* and *Sacrifice*, two B-grade action films. Only 60 people were on hand for the finale. The Hippodrome Theatre and the

empty office building above it met the wreckers' ball. Today a parking lot stands where the Hipp once drew the crowds.

The Embassy Theatre was located almost directly across Euclid Avenue from the Hippodrome. Its site had housed three previous theaters, the Columbia, Star, and Cameo theaters, all of which could be classified as houses for high burlesque. The Embassy, which actually retained the outer walls of these predecessors, was built with a completely new interior structure and designed as a motion picture theater. It opened on October 16, 1938, with the feature *Rich Man, Poor Girl*. Considerably less ornate than the more established downtown houses but with lots of chrome and velvet, the Embassy was also smaller, with seating for only about 1,200. Operated as part of the Community Circuit Theaters group, the Embassy's niche was to play second-run movies or first-run double-feature "B" films. That niche, however, must have been important, for the theater did rather well. The Embassy continued in business until

On a Sunday morning in 1951 lower Euclid Avenue was mostly empty. The marquee for the Tower Theatre can be see at the left, between the Clark's and Mills signs. *(Anthony Krisak photo, Jim Toman collection)*

The Embassy Theatre was just across the street from the Wm. Taylor and Sons department store.
(Jim Spangler collection)

December 1, 1977, closing only to make way for the National City Center development.

Another theater on lower Euclid Avenue, the Mall, was actually two theaters with lobbies that could be interconnected. The Lower Mall had an entrance on Superior Avenue and an auditorium seating about 600 people. The Upper Mall's entrance was at 303 Euclid Avenue. It had an auditorium and balcony seating about 1,000. At the time it opened in 1914, it was said to be the only theater in the country with two auditoriums, perhaps an early foreshadowing of today's multiplex houses.

Operating only briefly as a Loew's theater, the Mall spent most of its days as an independent house. As a result, the Mall theaters seldom hosted first-run movies, and those that it did were not likely to be box office hits. In the 1950s the Lower Mall began to show films "for mature audiences"

as a means of keeping the doors open. Titles such as *The Flesh and the Devil* and *Isle of Sinners* convey the type of fare rather succinctly. The Lower Mall's neighbor on Superior Avenue was the Women's Federal Savings and Loan Association, led by Lillian and Clara Westropp. Deeply religious women, they were appalled at the films screened next door. Women's Federal was a growing institution and needed room to expand, and so in 1957 the association bought the theater building, a purchase that served both a business purpose and a moral commitment. While the savings bank drew up plans for renovating the building, the theaters continued to operate. They screened their last films on August 31, 1960. The Upper Mall's final features were *Men on a String* and *Young Land*. The Lower Mall closed with *The Naked Road*, an unintentionally apt title, for it marked the end of the road for the two screens. The space occupied by the Lower Mall was converted into a parking garage, and the upper theater's space provided Women's Federal with a banking lobby on Euclid Avenue.

For a relatively brief period, lower Euclid hosted one other movie house, a late-comer to the avenue. The small Telenews Theater, with an auditorium which seated only 480, was located at 241 Euclid Avenue. It opened its doors on February 1, 1941. The newsreel was then a popular part of movie theater fare, and the operators of the Telenews believed, especially with war raging in Europe, that a venue that exclusively showed news features would have considerable appeal to a broad segment of the movie-going audience. So the Telenews created a format that featured a one-hour newsreel show that repeated throughout the day. Its opening presentation was *Salute to Cleveland*, a film highlighting several local achievements. After a few years of newsreels, the

operators changed the format to present longer films of the type that today might be seen on such cable networks as the Discovery Channel or the History Channel.

In 1950, as attendance began to slip, the operators again changed formats. The Telenews became the Coronet Theatre, and art films began to flicker on the screen. That experiment lasted only a few months. Then in 1951 the Telenews changed names yet again, becoming the Tower Theater. It was operated by the management of the Hippodrome. The Tower played double features. The Tower survived until February 25, 1954. Its last movie was *The Neanderthal Man*.

Lower Euclid Avenue did not have the glamor of the upper avenue, but it had variety and vitality, and its businesses managed to soldier on somewhat longer than the more celebrated establishments above East Ninth Street. Neither segment of Cleveland's Sophisticated Lady, however, was ultimately able to withstand the changing times.

This view from March 1956 indicates how shoppers crowded the sidewalks of the lower avenue. The scene is in front of The May Company. *(Cleveland* Press *Collection of the Cleveland State University Archives)*

VI

RECIPES
FROM THE AVENUE

T WO OF THE MOST POPULAR DINING SPOTS on Euclid Avenue were the Tea Room at Halle's and the two Stouffer restaurants. Perhaps the best way to remember these places would be to taste once again some of the fare that they served. The selection of recipes that follow will help you do just that. Each of the 22 recipes has been tested by our culinary consultants, Judith Karberg and Jane Hazen. Enjoy!

RECIPES FROM THE HALLE BROS. TEA ROOM

MINT BLACK BOTTOM PIE (*Makes two 9-inch pies*)

2 9" baked pie shells

Chocolate sauce (*See recipe below*)

2 quarts green mint or peppermint ice cream

Coat bottom and sides of pie shells with chocolate sauce. Spread half the ice cream over the bottom of the pie shells. Top with chocolate sauce, then with the remainder of the ice cream. Return to freezer for 2 hours. Top second half with chocolate sauce, and serve.

CHOCOLATE SAUCE (*Makes enough for two pies*)

2 cups granulated sugar

1/2 cup cornstarch

1/8 tsp. salt

2 cups water

4 ozs. chocolate, chopped

1/2 cup butter or margarine

2 Tbsp. vanilla

1/2 cup half and half

Melt butter and chocolate, and remove from heat. Combine sugar, cornstarch, and salt; then add water to make a smooth paste. Gradually stir this paste mixture into the melted butter/chocolate. Return to stove, and cook over low heat, stirring constantly. When sugar is completely dissolved, bring to a boil and continue stirring for two minutes. Remove from heat, and add vanilla. Divide chocolate sauce in half. Use one half to coat the bottom and sides of the two baked pie shells. To the second half, add the milk, and heat to blend. Cool, and use between the ice cream layers and on the tops of the pies.

❧ CLOUD NINE PIE *(Makes one 9-inch pie)*

1 9" graham cracker or gingersnap pie crust,
  well chilled
1½ cups vanilla ice cream

1½ cups chocolate ice cream
1½ cups green mint or peppermint ice cream

Spread first layer of ice cream evenly in pie shell, and place in freezer before adding successive layers. Keep in freezer until needed. Serve with hot fudge sauce and whipped cream.

❧ EGGNOG CHIFFON PIE *(Makes one 9-inch pie)*

1 envelope unflavored gelatin
½ cup granulated sugar
⅛ tsp. salt
1¾ cups dairy-made eggnog

3 eggs, separated
½ to 1 tsp. vanilla or rum extract
1 cup whipping cream
1 9" baked pie shell

Combine gelatin, ¼ cup of the sugar, and salt in the top of a double boiler. Stir in the eggnog. Place over boiling water, and stir until gelatin and sugar are dissolved. Beat egg yolks slightly, and quickly stir in a small amount of the hot gelatin mixture. Return the egg yolk mixture to the double boiler, and continue to cook until slightly thickened. Remove from heat, and add vanilla or rum extract. Chill until the mixture is slightly thicker than the consistency of unbeaten egg whites. Beat egg whites until stiff but not dry. Gradually beat in the remaining ¼ cup sugar. In a separate bowl, beat ½ cup of the whipping cream until stiff. Fold egg whites and cream into the gelatin mixture. Turn into baked pie shell, and chill until firm. Garnish with remaining whipped cream, maraschino cherries, and fresh green leaves.

Some of Halle's favorite dishes were served in the informal basement lunch room—1930s. *(Cleveland* Press *Collection of the Cleveland State University Archives)*

✇ PECAN PIE *(Makes one 9-inch pie)*

1 9" pie crust	2½ ozs. margarine (5 Tbsp.)
1½ cups plus 2 Tbsp. white corn syrup	1 cup plus 2 tsp. pecan pieces, chopped
½ cup plus 3 Tbsp. brown sugar, packed	3 Tbsp. honey
3 whole eggs	1 Tbsp. cake flour
1 egg white	20 to 30 pieces pecan halves
½ tsp. vanilla	

Whip together all ingredients, except the pecan halves, until well blended, and pour into raw pie shell. Put pecan halves on the top. Bake at 375 degrees for 10 minutes, then at 325 degrees for 1½ hours or until knife comes out clean. Serve with a dollop of whipped cream or ice cream.

✇ HALLE'S DATE NUT BREAD

¾ cup plus 1 Tbsp. plus 1½ tsp. granulated sugar	1½ tsp. baking powder
1 egg	2 cups plus 1 Tbsp. all-purpose flour
½ cup buttermilk	10½ ozs. dates, ground
½ cup hot coffee	1 cup plus 1½ tsp. pecan pieces
1½ tsp. baking soda	

Pour hot coffee over dates and set aside. Cream sugar and butter. Add eggs, and beat until well blended. Blend in the buttermilk. Add soda and baking powder to flour. Combine date mixture and nuts with liquid mixture. Add flour. Mix well and pour into a 9" x 5" x 3" greased and floured pan. Bake at 350 degrees for 50 minutes or until done.

✇ HALLE'S ALMOND RAREBIT *(Serves 5)*

4 Tbsp. butter	1 cup milk
4 Tbsp. flour	1 cup half and half
½ tsp. dry mustard	1 drop Tabasco sauce
1 tsp. salt	1 Tbsp. Worcestershire sauce
¼ tsp. paprika	½ lb. sharp cheese, grated

Melt butter in top of double boiler, and stir in next four ingredients. Stir in milk and half and half slowly until smooth and thickened. Add the Tabasco sauce, Worcestershire sauce, and cheese. Stir until lumps disappear. Pour over criss-crossed melba toast. Sprinkle generously with unbuttered, unsalted, toasted, blanched almonds.

ℛ FLUFFY FRUIT DRESSING *(Makes 1 quart)*

1 cup unsweetened pineapple juice

1/2 cup lemon juice

3 eggs, beaten

1 1/2 cups granulated sugar

3 cups whipped whipping cream

Mix fruit juices. Add eggs and sugar. Cook in top of double boiler until thickened. Cool. Fold in the whipped cream. Serve over fresh fruit.

ℛ CELERY SEED DRESSING *(Makes 1½ cups)*

3/4 cup granulated sugar

1 tsp. salt

1 tsp. dry mustard

1 tsp. paprika

1 tsp. celery seed

1/3 cup vinegar

1 tsp. grated onion juice

1 cup corn oil

Cook all ingredients, except onion juice and oil, on low heat until sugar is completely dissolved. Cool slightly. Blend in oil gradually, using an electric mixer. Add onion juice, and stir to blend. Store in refrigerator. Dressing is thick but will thin out on salad.

ℛ HALLE'S FRENCH DRESSING *(Makes 2¼ cups)*

1 cup vegetable oil

1/3 cup catsup

1/4 cup cider vinegar or wine vinegar

1/2 cup granulated sugar

1 clove garlic, minced

1 tsp. minced onion

1 egg

In blender combine oil, catsup, and vinegar. Add sugar, onion, and salt. Blend on low speed until well mixed, about 15 seconds. Add egg and garlic, and blend until smooth. Serve over fresh fruit or mixed salad greens.

NOTE: Tester did not use the raw egg, and the dressing was still delicious and had a good shelf life in the refrigerator.

This grilled entrance led into Halle's 7th floor Tea Room—c. 1920.
(Dixie Lee Davis collection)

HOLIDAY LOBSTER CASSEROLE

1 7-oz. package elbow macaroni	$1/2$ tsp. salt
3 cups lobster meat, cut up, cooked	$1/8$ tsp. pepper
3 Tbsp. lemon juice	$1/4$ tsp. dry mustard
2 Tbsp. butter	$1/4$ tsp. seasoned salt
1 Tbsp. grated onion	2 cups milk
$1/4$ cup green pepper, finely diced	2 cups American cheese, grated
1 4-oz. can of mushrooms, drained	$1/4$ cup dry sherry
2 Tbsp. all-purpose flour	Paprika to garnish

Cook macaroni as directed on label, and drain. Sprinkle lobster with lemon juice. Preheat electric frying pan to 260 degrees. Melt butter in frying pan, and saute onion, green pepper, and mushrooms. Blend in flour and seasonings. Gradually add the milk, stirring until mixture is smooth and thickened. Stir in $1^{1}/2$ cups of the cheese and the drained macaroni. Fold in the lobster and sherry. Sprinkle with remaining cheese and paprika. Cover frying pan, open vent, and bake at simmering point until hot and bubbly.

NOTE: Drained tuna, salmon, or other cooked fish may be substituted for the lobster.

Stouffer's, Play House
Square location.
(Courtesy of Nestlé USA, Inc.)

Stouffer's Luncheon and
Breakfast menus.
(Courtesy of Nestlé USA, Inc.)

RECIPES FROM STOUFFER'S

PAN CINNAMON ROLLS *(Makes 18)*

Dough:

$3/4$ cup water (65-70 degrees)	2 $1/3$ Tbsp. granulated sugar
$1/4$ cup nonfat dry milk	$1^3/4$ tsp. salt
(or substitute $3/4$ cup milk for water and dry milk)	1 egg
2 Tbsp. butter or margarine	1 envelope dry yeast
2 Tbsp. shortening	2 $1/2$ cups flour

Filling:

$1/4$ cup butter, melted	$1^1/2$ tsp. cinnamon
1 cup brown sugar	$1/4$ cup melted shortening

Glaze:

1 tsp. softened butter	$1/4$ tsp. fresh lemon juice
1 cup confectioner's sugar	$1/4$ tsp. grated lemon rind
2 Tbsp. half and half cream	

Pour water or milk into mixing bowl; add remaining dough ingredients, and blend thoroughly. Knead on a floured board until dough is elastic, about 15 minutes. Or use an electric mixer with a dough hook attachment, low speed for 10 to 15 minutes. Place dough in greased bowl, cover, and let rise until double in bulk, 1 to $1^1/2$ hours. Punch down, and let rest for 10 minutes. Roll into a rectangle 6" wide and $1/2$" thick. Combine melted butter, brown sugar, and cinnamon, and spread evenly over the dough. Fold one long side of the dough to the center; fold opposite side over the first fold, envelope style, and seal securely. Cut roll into $3/4$" slices. Place rolls $1/2$" apart in a greased 9" by 13" baking pan, cut side down, and brush with melted shortening. Let rise until double in bulk. Bake at 375 degrees for 18 to 20 minutes, until golden brown. Beat the glaze ingredients, and spread over warm rolls.

MARINATED THREE BEAN SALAD *(Serves 6)*

1 cup canned green beans, cut in $1/2$" lengths	$1/4$ cup cider vinegar
1 cup canned wax beans, cut in $1/2$" lengths	5 Tbsp. granulated sugar
1 cup canned red kidney beans, drained and rinsed	$1/2$ tsp. salt
$1/4$ cup chopped onion	$1/4$ tsp. pepper
$1/4$ cup salad oil	

Combine the beans and onion. Mix the rest of ingredients, and blend thoroughly. Pour dressing over beans, and toss. Cover and refrigerate overnight.

❧ VIENNESE CHICKEN SOUP *(Serves 4)*

2 Tbsp. margarine	2^1/$_3$ cups hot chicken broth
3^1/$_2$ Tbsp. flour	1^1/$_4$ cups hot half and half cream
^{1}/$_2$ tsp. salt	^{1}/$_4$ cup. finely chopped cooked chicken

Melt margarine in saucepan. Add the flour and salt, and whisk together; simmer 2 minutes to partially cook flour. Gradually add hot chicken broth, whisking constantly until smooth. Cook over medium heat until flour taste disappears. Add hot cream gradually, stirring constantly. Add cooked chicken, and heat through.

❧ HONEY GLAZED CARROTS *(Serves 4 to 6)*

1 lb. raw carrots	1 Tbsp. honey
1 Tbsp. butter, melted	^{1}/$_2$ tsp. salt
3 Tbsp. brown sugar	

Peel carrots, and cut into strips, ^{1}/$_2$" by 1/2" by 2^1/$_2$"; cook in boiling salted water until just tender, and drain well. Combine butter, brown sugar, honey, and salt in a heavy saucepan. Add drained carrots, and simmer 4 to 6 minutes, until glazed, stirring occasionally.

NOTE: A one pound bag of short cut carrots works fine, and saves time.

❧ BAKED CHICKEN AND BISCUIT *(6 servings)*

1^1/$_2$ cups biscuit mix	^{1}/$_2$ tsp. salt
^{1}/$_3$ cup cold water	1 drop yellow food coloring (optional)
6 Tbsp. shortening or margarine	2 whole chicken breasts, cooked and
^{1}/$_2$ cup all-purpose flour	cut into 2^1/$_2$" strips
3 ^{1}/$_4$ cups hot chicken broth	^{1}/$_2$ tsp. salt

Using a fork, stir biscuit mix and water until well blended. Roll to ^{1}/$_2$" thickness on a lightly floured surface, and cut into six biscuits, using a 3" cutter. Do not cut any thicker, or biscuits will be soggy. Refrigerate biscuits until needed. Melt margarine in a saucepan, blend in flour, and simmer 2 minutes, stirring. Gradually add hot chicken broth, beating constantly until smooth. Bring to a boil; reduce heat, and cook until gravy thickens. Add salt to taste, and a drop of yellow food coloring, if desired. Keep hot. Divide sliced chicken into six equal portions, and place in a greased 8" square baking pan. Sprinkle with salt. Pour hot gravy over chicken, and top each portion with a biscuit. Bake at 375 degrees for 30 to 35 minutes, or until golden brown.

LEMON ANGEL PIE *(One 10-inch pie)*

Crust:

4 egg whites, room temperature

1/3 tsp. cream of tartar

1 cup plus 1 1/2 Tbsp. granulated sugar, sifted

1 tsp. vanilla extract

Filling:

1 cup granulated sugar

1/4 tsp. salt

3 1/2 Tbsp. cornstarch

1 cup water

2 egg yolks, beaten

1/4 cup freshly squeezed lemon juice

1 1/2 cups sweetened whipped cream

Butter or spray with Pam one 10" pie plate, being sure to coat the rim. Beat egg whites until frothy; gradually add cream of tartar and sifted sugar, and beat until soft peaks form, and fold in vanilla extract. Place egg white mixture on bottom of pie pan (not up the sides). Mound slightly in the center. During baking, the meringue will rise up the sides of pan, and when removed from the oven, will fall into the natural pie crust shape. Bake at 300 degrees for 50 to 60 minutes or until a light golden brown and dry. Cool.

Meanwhile make the filling: Blend sugar, salt, and cornstarch together. Heat water to boiling in a heavy saucepan; gradually add sugar mixture, stirring constantly. Simmer until thickened and clear. Remove from heat. Add a small amount of the hot mixture to the egg yolks, and stir well. Return this mixture to saucepan, whisk together quickly, and return to low heat for a few minutes to cook yolks, stirring constantly. Blend in lemon juice and cool. Pour cooled filling over cooled crust. Mound whipped cream over filling. Sprinkle with nutmeg or grated lemon rind, if desired.

NOTE: This recipe was also excellent made with lime juice. It is best served immediately, as on sitting the meringue will start to soften. If you like, use aerosol whipped cream; this makes a decorative top for your pie, and if the new low fat whipped cream is used, you will have a very low fat dessert!

ROQUEFORT OR BLEU CHEESE DIP *(Makes about two cups)*

1 8-oz. package of cream cheese, room temperature

6 oz. crumbled Roquefort or bleu cheese

2 tsp. lemon juice

2 Tbsp. finely chopped onion

3/4 tsp. salt

1/2 cup half and half cream

Beat cream cheese until soft and creamy. Add all other ingredients except the cream, and beat to combine thoroughly. Add cream gradually; then refrigerate. Remove from refrigerator about 15 minutes before serving time. Serve with raw vegetables or crackers.

❧ SWISS APPLE FRITTERS *(Makes 1 to 1½ dozen)*

3 apples

1 cup flour

1 Tbsp. granulated sugar

1 tsp. baking powder

¼ tsp. salt

2 eggs, beaten

⅓ cup plus 2 Tbsp. milk

2 tsp. vegetable oil

oil for deep frying

sugar, cinnamon, or confectioner's sugar

Preheat oil to 375 degrees, or until bubbles form at the edge. Peel and core apples, and slice crosswise into rings, about ³/₈" thick. Use firm apples, and do not slice too thin; because the batter will be thick, thin slices will break. Mix flour, baking powder, sugar, and salt together. Mix eggs, milk, and oil in another bowl. Add to dry ingredients, and blend until smooth. Dip apple rings into batter, and allow some excess to drip back into bowl. Place rings in oil a few at a time, being careful not to crowd them. Fry for about 1½ minutes on each side, until nice and brown. Drain on paper towels. Mix cinnamon with either confectioner's sugar of granulated sugar. The confectioner's sugar is best sifted on; the granulated sugar can be placed in a small bowl and the warm rings can be dipped into it.

NOTE: These are really delicious! Because the batter is so thick, it is like a doughnut with an apple slice in the middle!

❧ WILLIAMSBURG ORANGE WINE CAKE *(Serves 12)*

½ cup soft butter

1 cup granulated sugar

2 eggs

1 tsp. vanilla extract

2 Tbsp. grated orange rind

1 cup seedless raisins

½ cup chopped walnuts

1½ cups flour

1 tsp. baking soda

½ tsp. salt

1 cup buttermilk

2 tsp. cream sherry

Cream butter well. Add sugar and cream about 5 minutes, until light and fluffy. Add eggs, and beat for another 3 to 5 minutes. Add vanilla, orange rind, raisins, and nuts, and mix thoroughly. Mix dry ingredients, and add alternately with buttermilk to the creamed mixture, beginning and ending with flour. Butter or spray with Pam a 9" by 13" pan. Pour batter in pan, and spread evenly. Bake at 350 degrees for about 25 minutes. Cool cake, brush with the cream sherry, and frost with Sherry Butter Cream Frosting (see below).

NOTE: The original recipe called for very long beating times. I assumed these directions were for hand mixing, and adjusted the mixing times for an electric mixer accordingly. The results were excellent!

℘ SHERRY BUTTER CREAM FROSTING

$\frac{1}{2}$ cup soft butter

$1\frac{1}{2}$ cups confectioner's sugar

4 tsp. cream sherry

Cream butter until fluffy. Add confectioner's sugar alternately with sherry, and beat until smooth and creamy. Spread on cooled cake.

℘ GRASSHOPPER PARFAIT *(Serves 6)*

$1\frac{1}{2}$ pints vanilla ice cream

$\frac{1}{2}$ cup white crème de cacao

$\frac{1}{2}$ cup green crème de menthe

$\frac{1}{2}$ cup sweetened whipped cream

6 fresh mint sprigs

Place 6 parfait glasses in the freezer until frosty. Assemble each parfait as follows:

1 small dip ice cream

1 tsp. crème de cacao

1 tsp. crème de menthe

1 small dip ice cream

1 tsp. crème de cacao

1 tsp. crème de menthe

1 small dip of ice cream

1 tsp. crème de cacao

1 tsp. crème de menthe

Freeze firm; allow to stand at room temperature 5 minutes before serving. Garnish each with whipped cream and a mint sprig.

EPILOG

Euclid Avenue, from Public Square to East 17th Street, was Cleveland's "Sophisticated Lady for a period of 50 years, from 1920 to 1970. Earlier the avenue had existed as a quiet residential street. Since the 1970s, however, the character of the avenue has been more tenuous and varied.

Cities are a human enterprise. As such, they reflect the ebb and flow of all human endeavors. Parts of cities, likewise, show cycles of development and decline. During the 1960s and 1970s the Erieview project revitalized Cleveland's once worn down East Ninth Street corridor. In the 1980s the old industrial Flats came alive as an entertainment district. In the 1990s the Warehouse District began to bloom as a residential area. But during these four decades, the glory that once marked Euclid Avenue faded away.

In the post-war years, life styles changed. In 1948, 493 million people moved around town on public transit. By 1970 the number had dropped to 115 million. In 1948 the city had but two express highways, the Shoreway and the Willow Freeway. By 1970 Greater Cleveland was laced with freeways stretching in all directions, and suburban shopping centers had multiplied. In 1950, 66% of Cuyahoga County residents lived within the city of Cleveland. By 1970, only 43% did so. These trends proved more forceful than the established dynamic of Euclid Avenue as the area's main shopping center could withstand.

Today the fortunes of Euclid Avenue have fallen on less than glorious times. In 2002 a trek along the famous street from Public Square to East 17th Street reveals a series of 40 empty store fronts, vacant office space above, a generally tired street scape, and only a smattering of pedestrians.

Today's Euclid Avenue does have its bright spots. The rebirth of Playhouse Square with its magnificently restored theaters, new buildings for Star Bank and the Wyndham Hotel, and the Star Plaza have infused new life into the area. Some office space, most notably the former Statler Office Tower, has been converted to residential use. On lower Euclid Avenue, the three arcades have been renovated and now are home to Marriott and Hyatt hotels. But, overall, these improvements have remained localized, and the avenue as a whole still lacks the vibrancy and sparkle of its glory days.

The demise of Euclid Avenue probably began with the closure of Taylor's in 1961. Taylor's was a medium-sized store, and the remaining larger stores had sufficient retail space to serve the public, yet there was an unsettling edge to the closure of a Cleveland institution.

The Taylor building was readily converted to office space which was then in great demand in the period prior to the building of Erieview and other projects.

The following decade marked a period when the floodgates opened and businesses of all kinds closed in seemingly rapid succession. Some downtown businesses relocated to suburban areas. Some firms found that they no longer fit the national trends, and they closed regardless of their location. In other cases entirely new shops replaced the old and familiar. Some were unique to the area, but an increasing number were part of large national firms. The era of the locally owned and managed establishment was nearing its end.

It is simplistic, however, to state that this decline occurred only in Cleveland. Many cities experienced the powerful trend towards suburbanization. The 1950s saw the development of the suburban shopping center as a serious alternative to downtown. Cleveland, of course, was a pioneer in the development of outlying shopping centers; Shaker Square, dating from 1927, is a case in point. But in the 1950s came Southgate, Westgate, and many smaller centers. The 1960s brought Parmatown and Severance, and the list continued to expand into the 1970s with the opening of Beachwood Place as the new stomping ground for the sophisticated shopper.

Instead of looking at this picture with sadness, it is probably wiser to understand

Scenes such as this one of Euclid Avenue at East Ninth Street depict the way it used to be—1926.
(Jim Spangler collection)

it as part of a continuum of change. The businesses on Euclid Avenue were themselves enterprises which had caused other older local firms to close their doors. Today in some cases the attractions of Beachwood Place survive tenaciously, unsure what the future holds. Although managers of these firms expend great energy trying to forecast upcoming trends and stay ahead of the competition, this perseverance does not always work. Firms close their doors and are quickly replaced by new ones.

Today many Greater Clevelanders look back of the glory years of Euclid Avenue with nostalgia. They loved Halle's, the confections at Boukair's, and the matinees at the Stillman. Perhaps someday people will look back fondly to the sparse decor of The Gap, the treats of a suburban mall food court, or the bazaar-like quality of a Dillard's main floor.

While we can remember the era of Euclid Avenue as Cleveland's Sophisticated Lady with nostalgia, we can also reflect on the standards of those days as we ponder what we should value and incorporate in our lives today. Do the displays at Sephora do justice to the tradition set by Taylor's? Does the delivery of merchandise from Abercrombie and Fitch in a homoerotic shopping bag match the quiet class of the green Halle bag? Does the person at a mall information kiosk provide the same level of polite competence as the doorman at a fine jewelry store?

And what of Euclid Avenue in the future? The rejuvenation of Euclid Avenue has been a main topic of city planning for

Saks Fifth Avenue and Beachwood Place seemed to draw the sophisticated shopper when downtown faded as the center for shopping, entertainment, and dining—2002. (Richard Karberg photo)

some time, going back at least to the mid-1980s when plans for what was then called the Dual Corridor project were being formulated. One iteration of that plan would have built a subway under Euclid Avenue from the Square to about East 18th Street.

From there a landscaped center reservation for electric light rail vehicles would have stretched to University Circle. The plan was to connect the city's two major employment hubs, the Square and the Circle, with a quick and convenient transit link and hopefully stimulate the redevelopment of commerce between the end points. City officials shelved that plan when it proved too expensive, but some of its chief features have been retained in a more recent but less costly version.

Today's scaled-back transit plan has the Greater Cleveland Regional Transit Authority promoting a Euclid Avenue bus-only center reservation with limited stops along the avenue. The entire route from Public Square eastward to the end of the transit line would be landscaped with trees and shrubs. Planners hope that the upgrade would stimulate the redevelopment of the upper stories of many of the largely vacant office buildings along Euclid into residential space and that this in turn would spur the return of retail trade to the Avenue.

Euclid Avenue made a smooth transition from a residential neighborhood for the wealthy to the city's commercial center. Will it emerge again as a prime residential street? Although no one can be certain, we can be optimistic. Hopefully Cleveland's famous main street will soon enter upon its third era of greatness.

And what has happened to the genteel lady who shopped the upper avenue? Does she now reside in Sedona instead of Cleveland? Does she yearn for the Beach Boys rather than the Dorsey Brothers? Has her fondness of sushi replaced the enjoyment of haute cuisine? Has her taste in films prioritized the Sundance festival instead of the drawing-room comedies presented by the Lunts?

The times change, and willing or not, we move ahead. Still, it is a pleasant thing to pause occasionally and remember older days. It gives us perspective—and inevitably a smile or two. And that is good.

FOR FURTHER READING

The following books add to the narrative presented here. Some have been helpful to the authors. Others may prove to be of interest to the reader.

Cigliano, J. (1991).
Showplace of America: Cleveland's Euclid Avenue,
1850-1910. Kent, OH:
Kent State University Press.

Condon, G. E. (1976).
Yesterday's Cleveland.
Miami: E. A. Seamann.

Deegan, G. and Toman, J. (1999).
The heart of Cleveland.
Cleveland: Cleveland Landmarks Press.

Herrick, C. (1986).
Cleveland Landmarks.
Cleveland: Cleveland Restoration Society.

Johanneson, E. (1979).
Cleveland architecture 1876-1976.
Cleveland: Western Reserve Historical Society.

Johanneson, E. (1983).
From town to tower.
Cleveland: Western Reserve Historical Society.

Karberg, R. (2000).
The Silver Grille: Memories and recipes.
Cleveland: Cleveland Landmarks Press.

Karberg, R. (2001).
The Higbee Company and the Silver Grille: More
memories and recipes.
Cleveland: Cleveland Landmarks Press.

Playhouse Square Cleveland:
An entertaining history. (2000).
Cleveland: Playhouse Square Association.

Rose, W. G. (1950).
Cleveland: *The making of a city.*
Cleveland: World.

Toman, J. and Cook, D. (1984).
Cleveland's changing skyline.
Cleveland: Cleveland Landmarks Press.

Van Tassel, D. and Grabowski J. (Eds). (1996).
The encyclopedia of Cleveland history. (2nd ed.).
Bloomington, IN: Indiana University Press.

Wilson, E. G. (1932, 1937).
Famous old Euclid Avenue.
Cleveland: World.

Witchey, H. R. (1994).
Fine arts in Cleveland.
Bloomington, IN: Indiana University Press.

Wood, J. M. (1987).
Halle's: Memoirs of a family department store.
Cleveland: Geranium Press.

INDEX OF ESTABLISHMENTS

INDEX OF ESTABLISHMENTS *(continued)*

INDEX OF RECIPES

LOCATION OF ESTABLISHMENTS - CIRCA 1950

THE LOWER AVENUE

1. Allen Theatre
2. Alpine Village
3. Arcade
4. B. R. Baker
5. Black Angus
6. Bond's
7. Bonwit Teller
8. Boukair's
9. Chef Hector's
10. Cikra's
11. Clark Restaurants
12. Cleveland Athletic Club
13. Cleveland Trust Building
14. Colonial Arcade
15. Colonnade
16. Cowell and Hubbard
17. Embassy Theatre
18. Engel and Fetzer
19. Euclid Arcade
20. F. W. Woolworth Company
21. Forum Cafeteria
22. Gazelle Restaurant
23. H. W. Beattie

24. Halle Bros. Company
25. Hanna Building / Restaurants
26. Hanna Theatre
27. Hermit Club
28. Hickory Grill Restaurant
29. Higbee Company
30. Hippodrome Theatre
31. Hotel Statler
32. Keith Building
33. Kornman's Restaurant
34. Lake Theatre
35. Mall Theatres
36. Mary Louise
37. May Company
38. Midday Club
39. Milgrim's

40. Mills Cafeteria
41. Nanking Restaurant
42. Ohio Theatre
43. Palace Theatre
44. Pat Joyce's
45. Peck and Peck
46. Pickwick Cafeteria
47. Pierre's Restaurant
48. Playhouse Square Restaurant
49. Richman Brothers Company

THE UPPER AVENUE

50. Rohr's
51. Rosenblum's
52. Rudolph Deutsch and Company
53. Russet Cafeteria
54. S. S. Kresge Company
55. Schofield Building
56. State Theatre
57. Stearn Company

58. Sterling Lindner Davis
59. Stillman Theatre
60. Stouffer Restaurants
61. Tavern Chop House
62. Telenews Theatre
63. Union Club
64. Union Trust Building
65. W. T. Grant Company
66. Webb C. Ball
67. Wm. Taylor & Sons
68. Williamson Building

SUPERIOR AVE.

CHESTER AVE.

E. 12TH ST.

E. 13TH ST.

CHESTER AVE.

E. 17TH ST.

HURON RD.

E. 14TH ST.

PROSPECT AVE.

N